A GUIDE TO STUDYING AND LIVING IN BRITAIN

More related titles

Critical Thinking for Students
Learn the skills of critical assessment and effective argument

'A really useful introduction to developing and improving a core skill.'
– Association of Commonwealth Universities Bulletin

How to Pass Exams Every Time
Proven techniques for any exam that will boost your confidence and guarantee success

'If you want a book that is excellently written and will show you how to study and approach exams, buy this!' – Amazon reviewer

Writing an Essay
Simple techniques to transform your coursework and examinations
'There is a lot of good sense in this book.' – *Times Educational Supplement*

The Best of London Parks and Small Green Spaces
Discover the often unknown delights of the green lungs of London
'Packed with surprising insights and discoveries . . . a fun, practical companion that can be referred to time and again.' – *What's on in London*

howtobooks

Send for a free copy of the latest catalogue to:

How To Books
3 Newtec Place, Magdalen Road,
Oxford OX4 1RE, United Kingdom
email: info@howtobooks.co.uk
http://www.howtobooks.co.uk

A GUIDE TO STUDYING AND LIVING IN BRITAIN

Up-to-date information and advice for international students in the UK

KRIS RAO

howtobooks

Published by How To Books Ltd,
3 Newtec Place, Magdalen Road,
Oxford OX4 1RE. United Kingdom.
Tel: (01865) 793806. Fax: (01865) 248780.
email: info@howtobooks.co.uk
http://www.howtobooks.co.uk

British Library Cataloguing in Publication Data
A catalogue record for this book is available from the British Library

Cover design by Baseline Arts Ltd, Oxford
Produced for How To Books by Deer Park Productions, Tavistock, Devon
Typeset by PDQ Typesetting, Newcastle-under-Lyme, Staffs.
Printed and bound by Bell & Bain Ltd, Glasgow

NOTE: The material contained in this book is set out in good faith for general guidance and no liability
can be accepted for loss or expense incurred as a result of relying in particular circumstances on
statements made in the book. The laws and regulations are complex and liable to change, and readers
should check the current position with the relevant authorities before making personal arrangements.

Contents

Preface   ix

Acknowledgements   x

1. Application   **1**
Benefits of British Higher Education   1
Choosing the right educational institution   3
The application process   5
Undergraduate courses   7
Postgraduate courses   8
English language requirements   9
Applying as a short-term visiting student   10
Glossary of educational terms   14
Useful addresses and contact details   15

2. General Information   **18**
Facts about the UK   18
British customs and habits   24
Money and banking   29
Post office services   32
Insurance   35
Utilities   36
Shopping   36
Discount cards   41
Time   42
Weights and measures   43
Telephone   43
Internet   49
Emergency services   49
Personal safety   50
Radio   50
Television   51
Newspapers and magazines   52
Eating out   54
Entertainment   55
Weather   58

Religion   58
Bank holidays   59
Drugs   59
Weapons   60

3. Travel   61
Travelling to the UK   61
Getting around the UK   65

4. Immigration   75
Passport or travel documents   76
How do I apply for a student visa/entry clearance?   78
Arriving in the UK   80
Police registration   83
Extending your student visa whilst in the UK   84
Visas to European (Schengen) countries   93
Visas to other European Union countries   105
Contacting your embassy for help   109

5. Health   116
National Health Service   117
Reciprocal healthcare agreements   118
Registering with a doctor   118
NHS Direct or NHS 24   119
Dentists and opticians   120
Pharmacies   121
Private health care   121
Counselling services   123
Vaccinations   123
Bringing health records to the UK   124
Health issues in the UK   124
Useful telephone numbers   126
Useful websites   126

6. Employment   **128**
    EEA nationals   128
    Non-EEA nationals/work permits   129
    Where to find work   130
    Wages   131
    Tax and National Insurance   131
    Employment rights   134
    Glossary of tax and NI terms   137
    Useful websites   137

7. Money   **140**
    Bringing money from home   141
    Bank accounts   141
    Building societies   143
    Glossary of banking terms   146
    Budgeting   148
    Financial difficulties   151
    What would it cost you?   151

8. University Life   **153**
    Settling in to university life   153
    Student support on campus   156
    Student media   157
    Study methods in British colleges and universities   161
    Graduation   163
    Religion   163
    Equality   163
    LGB groups   164
    Volunteering   164
    Sports and clubs   164
    Useful websites   166

9. Accommodation   **167**
    Halls of residence   167
    The host system   171
    Private shared accommodation   171

Repairs and maintenance   180
Glossary of accommodation terms   183
Useful websites   183

10. What Next?   **186**
Applying for another course   187
Staying on as a tourist or for graduation   187
Working in the UK after your studies   187
Students in Scotland   189
Storage   189
Sending goods back home   190
Reverse culture shock   194
Useful websites   195

Appendix – British universities and colleges   **196**

Further reading   **225**

Index   **227**

Preface

Some years ago, a confused international student approached me with several questions about student life in Britain. During the conversation I discovered that he'd had to scrounge for information to survive as a student in the UK. Later that evening, I walked into a bookshop to look for a guidebook on international student life in the UK – I couldn't find any. With the encouragement of my friends, I thought about writing one myself.

This book is the first of a series of guidebooks aimed at foreigners in the UK, and aims to answer questions about UK living. This book has come about as a result of my day-to-day interaction with several students, universities and government officials.

With its superb colleges and universities, Britain is a popular destination for international students. Currently, around 270,000 overseas students are studying at UK universities and the number is expected to rise by 10 per cent every year. In comparison to the United States or Australia, Britain offers a wider and richer experience to overseas students and a degree from Britain is recognised all over the world for its quality and academic strength.

A Guide Studying and Living in the UK will provide you with all the things you need to know about the British higher educational system and life in Britain. It includes information on the immigration regulations for students, university life, the health service, and British customs and traditions.

I hope you find this guidebook useful for your preparation to come to the UK and throughout the stay itself. Good luck!

Acknowledgements

This book has been a labour of love over many years of providing information, advice and guidance to others.

I am grateful to my good friends Canon Robin Crawford, Rev Peter Hannaway, Dr Adrian Winnett, Dr Ian Beadham and Kostas Nikoloudis who kept encouraging and nudging me to finish this book. I wish to thank my loving brother Rajiv Satya for his support.

Special thanks to Jenny Guildford for her invaluable help in correcting errors. Special thanks also to the staff and students at Reading University Students' Union, Reading University and the University of Bath.

Application

BENEFITS OF BRITISH HIGHER EDUCATION

A degree from Britain is renowned all over the world for its academic strength. British universities have been the training grounds for some of the greatest administrators, businessmen and scientists around the world. From Nehru to Lee Kuan Yew to Bill Clinton, many of those who have studied at British universities have proceeded to great careers. Employers worldwide appreciate the skills that British universities offer. Students also love British universities for their range of courses, flexibility, excellence, affordability, cosmopolitan cultural and social atmosphere. University campuses now have an international ambience as thousands of students from more than 150 countries come to Britain to study every year.

If you have looked into studying abroad, you may have considered other countries too. Studying in Britain is cheaper than studying in America. It is also easier to obtain a visa and clear immigration in Britain; anyone who goes through the American visa process in an American Consulate can attest to that. Britain offers a more cosmopolitan atmosphere than some American universities, which can be located in isolated areas. The British system also permits students to work outside the campus and also allows spouses to work, something that America doesn't allow.

Studying in the UK is good value for money because British degree programmes are more intensive and are generally shorter. A full-time undergraduate degree usually takes only three years to complete in the UK compared to four years in the United States or Australia. A full-time postgraduate (masters) course in the UK can take only one year to complete compared to two in the United States or Australia (although some are also two years in the UK).

Britain also offers greater employment opportunities than other Commonwealth countries like Australia and New Zealand. Britain is a link to both Europe and America and you will find more companies recruiting in Britain than Australia and New Zealand.

However, to derive the maximum benefit for your career, you should look at your choice. There are thousands of subjects to choose from and an array of academic and vocational levels from school-leaving qualifications to undergraduate and postgraduate degrees. There are also many competing universities and courses, which may or may not meet your requirements. You may be able to get a place at a prestigious institution but your choice of course is also important.

CHOOSING THE RIGHT EDUCATIONAL INSTITUTION

Higher educational institutions in Britain are classified as private colleges, colleges of further education, colleges of higher education and universities.

Private colleges offer courses that prepare students for professional and technical courses as well degree courses. Their fees are usually high because they do not get any government funding. There are a lot of private colleges springing up around Britain. Before you apply, check whether they are accredited by the independent British Accreditation Council. Their website (www.the-bac.org) has a list of the accredited private colleges.

Colleges of further education (CFE) offer a vast range of professional, vocational and qualification courses including GCSEs, AS, A levels, access courses, BTEC and GNVQs. They also include sixth form colleges, technical colleges, arts and technology colleges and colleges of education in Scotland.

Colleges of higher education (CHE) usually offer courses leading to degrees, postgraduate qualifications, professional and vocational qualifications and diplomas of higher education. They include colleges of further education, institutes of higher education as well as schools and academies of music and drama.

Universities offer higher educational qualifications (diploma, degree, masters and doctoral) as well as other professional qualifications.

Choosing what and where to study can be difficult. You should go through prospectuses carefully and compare the different colleges/universities before you decide on your course. You can obtain a prospectus by writing to the universities' admissions office or to their international office. You may also be able to obtain a prospectus from the British Council office or the local recruitment office of the university. Alternatively, most educational institutions now have a downloadable prospectus on their website. The Universities and Colleges Admissions Service (UCAS) website has complete links to all colleges, colleges of further education and colleges of higher education (see www.ucas.ac.uk). Universities UK, an association of British universities, also has links for all the universities in the UK on their website www.universitiesuk.ac.uk. A detailed directory of universities and colleges in the UK can be found in the Appendix of this book.

Before deciding on an institution, check the environment/location, the cost of living in that area, the number of international students, the teaching methods, and the student-to-lecturer ratio. Your local British Council or an admissions officer at the college or university will be able to help you with these details. Those applying for an undergraduate degree course can also check with Universities and Colleges Admissions System (UCAS) before applying.

Although there is no official ranking of the universities or colleges in the UK, *The Sunday Times* and the *Guardian* newspaper offer a useful guide to British Universities and list different departments in order of rank. *The Sunday Times* and the *Guardian* league tables of British universities and colleges is compiled using a formula that rewards teaching excellence and the academic standard of admissions above all else. Use this guide in conjunction with individual university prospectuses.

The Sunday Times *university rankings for 2005*
1. University of Oxford
2. University of Cambridge
3. Imperial College, London
4. London School of Economics
5. University of Warwick
6. University College, London
7. University of York
8. University of Durham
9. University of St Andrews
10. University of Loughborough

The Guardian *ranking of British universities for 2005*
1. University of Oxford
2. University of Cambridge
3. Imperial College, London
4. School of Oriental and African Studies
5. London School of Economics
6. King's College, London
7. University College, London
8. University of York
9. University of Warwick
10. University of Edinburgh

THE APPLICATION PROCESS

Applying to most of the educational institutions in the UK is simple and straightforward. You can apply to some institutions online. Check the institution's website to see whether they permit online applications. You can also request an application pack and return your application by post.

The British Council

The British Council offices around the world offer free guidance to students wishing to study in Britain. The British Council has direct contacts with academic institutions in Britain. The Council offices will have a range of prospectuses and course details of academic institutions in the UK. The counsellors at the British Council can also assist students with their enrolment and give further guidance on visa, funding and accommodation matters.

Private recruiters

Many British universities have official agents working on their behalf in many countries around the world. These agents are usually trained educational counsellors and can assist students with enrolment procedures. Most agents offer their services free of charge (they receive commission for every student enrolled) although some may charge a fee. Many of these referral agents are listed in your local *Yellow Pages*. You may also come across their adverts in your local newspaper.

Courses in colleges

To enrol on a college course you need to apply directly to the college admissions officer. When applying, make sure you write a covering letter giving all the necessary information and your contact details. Before applying for a course check that the institution is accredited by the British Accreditation Council (see page 3). If you are a non-EEA national, then the visa officer or immigration officer may want to know this before issuing a visa. Entry clearance officers at British missions abroad will only grant visas to prospective students of educational institutions listed in the Register of Education and Training Providers (compiled by the Department for Education and Skills). You can search for them at www.dfes.gov.uk/providersregister. Remember to verify your college before you apply for a visa.

UNDERGRADUATE COURSES

UCAS system
All students applying to study for an undergraduate degree in the UK will have to go through the UCAS (Universities and Colleges Admission System). UCAS is an independent body that offers impartial and up-to-date information on higher education courses, colleges and universities. All colleges and universities that are in the UCAS scheme are recognised by the British government.

The quickest and easiest way to apply is online through the UCAS website (www.ucas.ac.uk). Alternatively, you can get an application form from your local British Council office, local agent of the University or by writing directly to UCAS at UCAS, Rosehill, New Barn Lane, Cheltenham GL52 3LZ, UK. You can also order applications forms from their website. You can use one application form to apply to up to six universities. Completed application forms need to go back to UCAS with the required payment (£5 if you are applying for one university and £15 for 2–6 universities).

If you are applying from within the UK/EU, your application should arrive at UCAS between 1 September and 15 January of the previous academic year except for courses at Oxford or Cambridge University, or for courses in medicine, dentistry and veterinary science.

If you are applying from outside the UK/EU you are given extra time and you can apply any time between 1 September and 30 June, except for courses at Oxford or Cambridge University or for courses in medicine, dentistry, and veterinary science. However, courses get filled very quickly, so it is best to apply as early as possible. This will also give you plenty of time to make arrangements for your visa (for non-EEA nationals only), accommodation, finances and travel arrangements.

UCAS will acknowledge each of your applications within six weeks, and in another six weeks you will be notified of the success of your application from each of your chosen institutions. Depending on the outcome you will receive an unconditional offer, a conditional offer, or a rejection.

Clearing

UCAS runs a special service called 'clearing' during August and September. All available places in courses that have not been filled are listed. Late applications may be eligible to go through the clearing process.

POSTGRADUATE COURSES

For postgraduate courses you need to apply directly to the department's admissions tutor. You will find the name and address of this person in the university prospectus, or alternatively you can apply directly to the international office who can organise things for you. You can apply for as many different courses in different universities as you wish. Apply early, however, as some courses will get filled very quickly. Remember that it also takes time to arrange references, supporting documents and funding.

Full time or part time

Educational institutions offer students the chance to complete
their course either full time or part time. EEA nationals can study
part time. However, non-EEA nationals are not permitted to
study in the UK on a part-time basis if they are in the UK on a
student visa/entry clearance. Part-time course fees are a lot
cheaper, but the courses take longer to complete.

ENGLISH LANGUAGE REQUIREMENTS

International students are required to demonstrate a good
command of the English language as an admission requirement
for all academic courses. The requirements are usually in the form
of two most widely accepted qualifications – International English
Language Testing Service (IELTS) or Test of English as a Foreign
Language (TOEFL). These qualifications are offered by various
institutions around the world. Some educational institutions in the
UK accept other English Language Tests or qualifications, but
these may vary. Check with an institution before you apply. Most
educational institutions ask for an IELTS score of 6.0 or a
TOEFL score of around 550 (or around 230 if you take the new
computer-based tests).

Please note that these requirements do not apply if your first
language is English, or if you can provide evidence that your
education in your home country was conducted in an English
medium.

Most educational institutions in the UK also have their own in-
house IELTS testing centre. If you have not sat this exam, or your
IELTS or TOEFL score fell below the required level, you might be
asked to complete a short course of around 150–400 hours of

English tuition before being formally accepted for an academic course.

APPLYING AS A SHORT-TERM VISITING STUDENT

Non-EU visiting students

In the top universities enrolment is competitive and places are limited. It is best to start your application at least one year before you are planning to start a course. The deadline for applications is usually the second week of May for the summer and autumn terms, and the second week of October for the spring term.

Once you have decided on a university, contact their study abroad programme co-ordinator for an application form and an information pack. Complete the application form and return it to the study abroad office, together with the transcripts of your current university studies and academic references. If you are selected, they will send you a letter of offer and a course catalogue. Use this catalogue to choose the course/module you would like to take. You should also discuss your course choice with your tutor at home to ensure that it meets your course requirements and transfers.

If you need further information on classes you can contact the study abroad adviser in an individual department by email or telephone. Fill in the class details and send it back to the study abroad office. You will then be sent a letter of acceptance. A few weeks before you are due to arrive the study abroad office will also send you details about your accommodation and other details about your arrival.

EU students

EU students are chosen by their home universities to participate in particular study programmes abroad and must apply through their home university. British universities have agreements with many EU universities for student exchange under the Socrates–Erasmus programme.

Usually the course is valued in terms of the ECTS (European Course Transfer System). An academic year is made up of 60 ECTS credits with a term equalling 20 ECTS credits. Check with your home university whether this meets your academic requirements.

Each student will be required to complete a learning agreement and an enrolment form. You will then receive a letter of offer.

Fees

All non-EU students have to pay higher tuition fees than UK students, because their study is no longer subsidised by the British Government. EU nationals are comparatively better-off because they pay the same fees as UK students. The rates of fees vary from institution to institution and according to the subjects studied. Science-based subjects are more expensive than arts or social science-based subjects. More specialised qualifications like medicine or dentistry are also more expensive.

The table below gives a rough idea of fees charged by educational institutions each year in the UK.

	EU students	Non-EU students
Degree (full time)	up to £3,000*	£8,000–£11,000
Postgraduate (full time)	£3,000	£9,000–£15,000
Non-degree professional courses	£2,500–£8,000	£4,500–£10,000

* The amounts charged will vary between courses and universities and colleges.

Scholarships

There is limited funding available for overseas students in the UK. EEA students are permitted to apply for financial assistance in order to cover tuition fees on the basis of low income from the Department of Education and Employment. You can email EUTeam@dfes.gsi.gov.uk for an application pack or contact them directly on 01325 391 199. You will need to fill in the form and supply proof of your parental income. If you are eligible for funding your fees will then be paid directly to your educational institution. Check www.dfee.gov.uk for further details. EEA students can also obtain additional funding from their government or other funding bodies in their home country. Scholarships are also available from some universities and colleges.

Very limited government scholarships are available to non-EEA students and scholarships for undergraduate courses are even rarer. Some of these are:

British Chevening Scholarships

These scholarships are funded by the Foreign and Commonwealth Office, and are given to around 2,200 overseas students planning to study a post-graduate course. This scholarship can be awarded as a full award where fees, living allowance and travel expenses are paid; a fees-only award; and a combination of both. Contact the British Council or the embassy or high commission in your home country for further details.

Commonwealth Scholarships and Fellowship Plan
These are given mainly to students on postgraduate courses from a Commonwealth country only. Applications have to made in your own country through the Commonwealth Scholarship Agency or local British Council offices.

DFID Shared Scholarship Scheme
This scheme is mainly aimed at postgraduate courses and is awarded by the Department of International Development and some universities to students from a developing Commonwealth country. There are some restrictions on age, subjects and your employment status. Contact the British Council or the embassy or high commission in your home country for further details.

Overseas Research Awards Scheme
Funded by the Department of Education and Skills, this scholarship is given to postgraduate research students who demonstrate exceptional academic and research merit. Applications can be made through the university at which you study.

University scholarships
Several UK universities offer scholarships to both EEA and non-EEA students. Their details are usually listed in the prospectus and on their website. However, do bear in mind that these scholarships are limited and are based on merit.

Other scholarships
There are several private scholarships available for overseas students (both EEA and non-EEA). Hobsons' *Sponsorship and Funding Directory* published annually has details about private companies offering scholarships. Prospects' *Funding Guide* is another good guide with plenty of information on private and public funding bodies in the UK.

www.britishcouncil.org
The British Council site has links and further information on the main scholarship schemes offered by the British government and British colleges and universities.

www.educationuk.org/scholarships
The Education UK website has an easy-to-use search facility for scholarships, bursaries and awards. The search facility lets you choose awards relating to course, institution and charity or organisation.

www.prospects.ac.uk
This website has complete details about postgraduate opportunities in the UK including sources of funding.

GLOSSARY OF EDUCATIONAL TERMS

BA: Bachelor of Arts
BSc: Bachelor of Science
BSocSc: Bachelor of Social Science
DLitt: Doctor of Literature
FE: Further Education
GCSE: General Certificate of Secondary Education
GNVQ: General National Vocational Qualification

HE:	Higher Education
HND:	Higher National Diploma
IELTS:	International English Language Testing Service
MA:	Master of Arts
MPhil:	Master of Philosophy
MSc:	Master of Science
NCVQ:	National Council for Vocational Qualifications
PGCE:	Postgraduate Certificate of Education
PhD:	Doctor of Philosophy
SCOTVEC:	Scottish Vocational Educational Council
SVQ:	Scottish Vocational Qualification
SWAS:	Social Work Admissions Systems
TEFL:	Teaching English as a Foreign Language
TOEFL:	Test of English as a Foreign Language
UCAS:	Universities and Colleges Admission System
UCLES:	University of Cambridge Local Examinations Syndicate

USEFUL ADDRESSES AND CONTACT DETAILS

British Accreditation Council
Westminster Central Hall, Storey's Gate
London SW1H 9NH
Tel: 020 7233 3468
www.the-bac.org

British Council
Information Centre
10 Spring Gardens
London SW1A 2BN
Tel: 020 7930 8466
Fax: 020 7839 6347
www.britishcouncil.org

Department for Education and Employment
Sanctuary Buildings
Great Smith Street
London SW1P 3BT
Tel: 020 7925 5000
Fax: 020 7925 6000
www.dfee.gov.uk

UCAS (Universities and Colleges Admissions Service)
Rosehill, New Barn Lane
Cheltenham GL52 3LZ
Tel: 01242 222 444
www.ucas.org.uk

UKCOSA (United Kingdom Council for Overseas Student Affairs)
9–17 St Albans Place
London N1 0NX
Tel: 020 7226 2762
www.ukcosa.org.uk

USEFUL WEBSITES
www.the-bac.org
The British Accreditation Council website lists all the independent colleges of further and higher education. It also has a database of all of the accredited colleges in the UK.

www.universitiesuk.ac.uk
Universities UK is an association of UK universities. The site has links to all the universities in the UK.

www.educationuk.org

A comprehensive website containing information about all aspects of studying in the UK. The site offers a search facility for individual courses, colleges and universities.

www.britishcouncil.org

The British Council website has links and further information about colleges and universities in the UK. The site also provides information and guidance on applying for courses in the UK.

www.prospects.ac.uk

This website has complete details about postgraduate opportunities in the UK including sources of funding.

www.ucas.org.uk

The UCAS website has details on applying for undergraduate courses in the UK. The site also permits you to apply online and check the status of your application.

www.ukcosa.org.uk

UKCOSA is an independent organisation that promotes the interests of overseas students in the UK. The website has information, advice and useful links for all prospective and current students in the UK.

General Information

FACTS ABOUT THE UK

Nestled on the north western corner of Europe, the United
Kingdom (UK) is a small island country between the North Sea
and the Atlantic Ocean. With an area of around 242,000 sq km
(93,000 sq miles), the UK is about as large as the American state
of Colorado or the African country of Guinea. It is no more than
1,000 km (about 600 miles) from the southern coast to the
northern tip of Scotland and is less than 500 km (300 miles) wide.
The country's official name is the United Kingdom of Great
Britain and Northern Ireland. The island of Great Britain
comprises England, Scotland and Wales. Northern Ireland is the
area in the north eastern corner of Ireland, an adjacent island.
The UK is one of the 25 member states of the European Union
(EU). The English Channel separates Britain from the European
continent.

Map of the British Isles and Ireland.

The UK's total population of 60 million is unevenly distributed, with 5 million people living in Scotland, 3 million in Wales, 2 million in Northern Ireland and the majority of 50 million people in England. The population density of the UK is around 246 people per square kilometre with England the most densely populated, with around 383 people per square kilometre. Nearly one third of the people in England live in the South East (an economically rich area) and in London, the capital.

Britain has a milder climate than most of northern and eastern Europe owing to the warm Gulf Stream in the Atlantic Ocean. However, it is regarded as a wet country. The temperature is rarely over 30°C (85°F) or below 0°C (32°F), the average temperature is 4°C in winter and 16°C in summer. It gets colder in Scotland, Wales and Northern parts of England. However, you will never experience the bitter cold months and scorching summers of other countries.

Geographically England is mostly rolling land, rising to the uplands of southern Scotland. Central Scotland also has lowlands. The northern coast has granite highlands.

People
Today, Britain has a diverse population with immigrants from every continent and country. Most people in England are English, descendants of Anglo-Saxons, the people who first came and settled from Germany and Scandinavia about 1,500 years ago. The Irish, Welsh and Scottish are descendants of the Celts (pronounced Kelts), who inhabited Britain before the Anglo-Saxons came. The ethnic minorities of Britain are Asians from the

Indian sub-continent and China, Arabs from North Africa and Middle East, Africans and Caribbean islanders, and people from Eastern Europe.

In general, the UK is an open-minded, well-educated, and tolerant society, and ethnic differences have sparked little violence or hostility. As a foreigner you are also covered by legal protection. The Race Relations Act 1976 made it illegal to discriminate against any person because of race, colour, nationality or origin.

Language

English is the most widely used language in Britain, the official language of the government and the first language of most of its citizens. There are many types of English accent across the United Kingdom, some of which are incomprehensible to the foreigner. It may benefit you to get the feel of the local accent in the area in which you intend to study. Other languages in the UK include Scottish Gaelic, Irish Gaelic and Welsh. Some cities with large Asian populations also recognise Indian languages like Gujarati, Punjabi and Bengali.

Culture

Since the time of William Shakespeare, about four hundred years ago, Britain has been a fountain of culture. London's West End has some of best plays in the world. There are about 300 professional theatres producing plays and the UK hosts around 600 professional arts festivals each year. Britain is also the home of the Beatles and many famous bands and musicians. Some of the world's best libraries and museums are to be found in Britain, mainly in London. The British Museum is distinguished for its extensive and diverse collections, from Egyptian mummies to important historical documents. The National Gallery features a vast collection of British and European paintings dating from the 13th century to modern times. The National Portrait Gallery has about 10,000 portraits of famous figures from British history, some dating from the 14th century. The Victoria and Albert Museum houses one of the world's largest collections of fine and applied arts, from jewellery, clocks, and pottery to fabrics, furniture, and musical instruments.

Government

On paper, the UK is a monarchy, ruled by a king or queen: you will see the royal insignia on most government documents. In practice, however, the Prime Minister is the real head of government. Voters elect their members of parliament (MPs) to the House of Commons at Westminster in London who in turn select a prime minister. There are 646 MPs each representing the people of their constituency. The House of Lords has some hereditary peers, life peers and bishops (although hereditary peers may be replaced by elected peers in the future). There are three main parties: the Labour party, the Conservatives and the Liberal Democrats. The British Prime Minister Tony Blair has been running the country under the Labour party for the last ten years.

Economy

The UK has currently one of Europe's booming economies but this hasn't always been the case. In the Seventies there were chronic strikes and unemployment. But the government's policy of freeing industry from oppressive regulations and encouraging competition has yielded great dividends. Today the unemployment rate is very low compared to France or Germany. The service sector employs roughly 75 per cent of the work force, manufacturing about 20 per cent, agriculture 2 per cent and fishing and mining a mere 1 per cent each. The City of London is one of the world's leading financial centres. Banking, finance and insurance account for about 12 per cent of Britain's GDP and employ more than a million people. Britain is also a prominent tourist destination, with around 25 million foreign visitors a year. Tourism is an important industry in Britain employing 1.8 million people and accounting for approximately 5 per cent of the GDP.

Culture shock

It can be a cultural shock to find yourself in unfamiliar surroundings, when familiar sights, sounds, smells and patterns of behaviour are replaced by strange and different experiences.

At the time of your departure and arrival you may begin to feel anxious or unhappy. This is quite normal. Many of you may also feel excited – there is a lot happening, lots to do and the excitement can carry you along in a 'honeymoon' stage for a few days or more. But after that time you may start to miss friends and family, get tired of the weather, scenery or food and tired of the effort you have to make with perhaps a different language or simply different patterns of behaviour. At this time it can be a good idea to socialise with people from your own part of the world and keep in touch with your family and friends back home. The support facilities at your college or university can also help.

The counsellors, advisers, nurses and chaplains at your college or university are all experienced and skilled at helping with the process of culture shock. For most people, support at this time helps them to absorb their experiences, and learn to be 'bicultural', by operating in both their new and their traditional cultures. Dealing with culture shock can be a valuable learning experience giving you skills that will serve you well in later life.

BRITISH CUSTOMS AND HABITS

Queuing

Queuing is a feature of British life that seems to fascinate visitors. If you have not witnessed 'queuing' before, it is simply the way in which people form a line (as children do in most primary schools) in a shop or when they buy a ticket etc., with the intention of allowing those who arrive first to be served first. It is advisable to take your place in the queue and not to push your way to the front, as this may annoy other people in the queue. If you are really in a desperate hurry, people will almost always let you through to the front if you just ask politely.

Forms of greeting

All cultures have unspoken/unwritten rules about how to behave when you meet someone. It is not possible to go into all the different forms of appropriate behaviour here, but in Britain it is normal to shake hands when you meet someone, especially for the first time. This is acceptable for both men and women. In Britain, unlike some other European countries, it is not usual to embrace or kiss the other person (unless they are family or a very close friend).

You may find it unusual that the British address other people by their first names, particularly if your own culture uses more formal terms of address. It is quite normal for students, for instance, to address their tutors or other members of staff (including professors) by their first names. However, if you feel more comfortable using surnames when talking to members of staff, then it is quite all right to do so. If people are called by their last name then this is preceded by the titles Mr (for men) and Ms (for women). Some women will prefer to be called Mrs (for married women) or Miss (unmarried), but Ms is usually now quite commonly used, unless corrected by the woman in question.

Please/Thank you/Sorry

These words are the most used (perhaps over-used) in the English language. In some cultures it is appropriate to say 'thank you' if, perhaps someone has just saved your life, but in Britain it is normal to say 'thank you', 'please' etc. for seemingly small things. There are no absolute rules about where and when you use these polite terms, but you should certainly use them when shopping, addressing strangers or on public transport. Even in the home, family members will use 'thank you' and 'please' with one another and it would be considered rude not to. British feel more comfortable when these words and phrases are introduced into conversation than if they are omitted.

Punctuality

Be aware of the British attitude to promptness and keeping appointments. It is considered impolite to be late or to miss an appointment. If you have made an arrangement and you have been delayed and/or cannot make the appointment, then do make an effort to contact the person to let them know. In certain cases, (for example, dentists' appointments) you may be charged for the missed appointment if you do not give sufficient notice of cancellation (usually 48 hours).

Making friends

British people are generally friendly but relationships may take some effort at first. Women in Britain are independent and are accustomed to entering public places unaccompanied. The best way to make friends is to start chatting to people on your course or where you are staying, over a cup of tea or coffee and to join in the activities and societies offered by your Students' Union.

Visiting others

It is customary in Britain for invitations to visit someone's house to be for a prearranged time and day. As a generalisation most people are not comfortable if people just drop in, and in most houses the front door is kept closed. However, if someone suggests you drop round any time, you should not feel worried about doing so as long as it is not in the middle of the night.

Slang words

You can get by in Britain if you can speak and understand standard English. But to make yourself feel completely at home, you need to have some knowledge of the British 'slang'. Spoken English in Britain contains many non-standard words and phrases, whose meaning is not clear to an untrained visitor. Here are some of the slang words that you will probably encounter during your stay as a student:

Slang words

All right?:	'Hello, how are you'? (a form of greeting)
Aye:	Yes (in Scotland)
He went ballistic:	He went mad
Bangers:	Sausages
Bloke:	Male
Brilliant:	Great or awesome

Bladdered:	Drunk
Blimey:	An expression of surprise
Blinding:	Great
Bloody:	Word generally used for emphasis
Bollocks:	Rubbish
It cost a bomb:	It was expensive
Chips:	French fries
Copper:	Policeman
Chat up:	To be flirtatious
Cheesed off:	Upset
Cock up:	Mistake
Cracking:	Good
Crikey:	Another exclamation of surprise
What's the damage:	What will it cost?
Dosh:	Money
Daft:	Stupid
Dim:	Stupid
Dodgy:	Bad quality or untrustworthy
Dull:	Boring
Fancy:	Like or desire
She or he's fit:	She or he's good looking
Flog:	Sell
Fortnight:	Two weeks
Geezer:	An old man
Git:	An undesirable person
Grub:	Food
Gutted:	Sad or upset
Haggle:	Barter or negotiate
Jolly good:	Very good
Kip:	A short nap
Knackered:	Tired

Loaded:	Very rich
Loony:	Mad or crazy
Mate:	A friend
Mug:	Naive
Naff:	Uncool
Na:	No (in Scotland)
Nice one!:	A compliment on a job well done
Nick:	Steal
Pants:	Bad
It was peanuts:	It was cheap
Piece of cake:	Easy
Pissed:	Drunk
Pissing around:	Fooling about
Plastered:	Drunk
Posh:	High class
Puke:	Vomit
Pukka:	Super
Quid:	A pound (currency)
Shag:	To have sex
Snog:	Kiss
Ta:	Thanks (short form)
Taking the mickey:	Making fun of
Taking the piss:	Making fun of
Up for it:	To be available
Uni:	University (short form)
Wind up:	Making fun of
Wee:	Little/small (in Scotland)
Wicked:	Great

Business hours
Offices are generally open from 9am to 5pm Monday to Friday. However, shops are open later and are also open at the weekends.

MONEY AND BANKING

Money
The currency in the UK is the pound sterling (£). There are one hundred pence (p) to a pound (£1 = 100p). Coins come in denominations of 1p, 2p, 5p, 10p, 20p, 50p, £1 and £2. All coins bear the Queen's head on one side, but have different flip-sides, marking the different countries of Britain: three lions for England, a thistle or Forth Bridge for Scotland and a leek or dragon for Wales etc.

Notes come in denominations of £5 (green), £10 (brown), £20 (purple) and £50 (red). Banks in Scotland and Northern Ireland issue their own currencies in denominations of £1, £5, £10, £20, £50 and £100. Most shops accept these currencies but if they are refused you can exchange them at a bank.

Changing money
You can change money and travellers' cheques at any Bureau de Change on the high street, in some travel agents, and at banks or some major post offices.

Be warned that the commission on these transactions can be high in some places (around 2 per cent with a minimum of £2). Check the exchange rate and any commission charges in advance. Many banks and post offices have abolished commission on all foreign exchange transactions and offer good exchange rates. Most travel agents such as Thomas Cook and Going Places also exchange foreign currencies commission-free. If you have a student bank account you can usually change your money commission-free at your bank.

Exchange rates (correct as of 14 May 2005)
The following is a brief guide to the current exchange rates. Please note that exchange rates are subject to change and fluctuate daily. For real time rates check online at www.reuters.co.uk/currencies.jhtml

1 GBP	=	2.34	Australian Dollars
1 GBP	=	4.68	Brazilian Real
1 GBP	=	2.18	Canadian Dollars
1 GBP	=	15.67	Chinese Yuan (RMB)
1 GBP	=	1.47	Euros
1 GBP	=	82.47	Indian Rupees
1 GBP	=	196.24	Japanese Yen
1 GBP	=	144	Kenyan Shillings
1 GBP	=	18.86	Mexican Pesos
1 GBP	=	2.59	New Zealand Dollars
1 GBP	=	253.61	Nigerian Naira
1 GBP	=	12.02	South African Rand
1 GBP	=	1.76	US Dollars

Transferring/receiving money
The quickest way to send or receive money is by using Western Union (0800833833 or www.westernunion.co.uk) or Moneygram (0800 8971 8971 or www.moneygram.com). You can transfer money at main post offices around the UK. Money Gram has relatively few offices in the UK but Western Union has entered into a franchise agreement with many local shops, travel agents and bureaux de change in Britain. It takes around three minutes

to send or receive money worldwide using these services. However, the commission charges are usually high.

An International Bank Draft is the cheapest way to send or receive money. To send a draft, simply go to your branch and specify the bank branch, the city and the country you want the money to be sent to. A draft for the amount will be issued after debiting your account. You'll then need to post this draft to the receiver. If payment is urgent you can send or receive money directly to your bank account by telegraphic transfers. Telegraphic transfers from bank to bank can take up to three days and cost around £15. Foreign cheques take a long time (around three to four weeks) to clear and are subject to high commission charges.

Banking systems

Banks and building societies in the UK are generally open from 9.30am to 5.00pm, Monday to Friday, and some are open 9.30am to 12 noon on Saturday. High street branches operate full banking facilities including a bureau de change, while branches at universities or colleges usually offer limited facilities.

Cash machines/ATMs

There are plenty of cash machines available in shopping areas and there are also likely to be some on your university or college campus. Almost all bank cards issued around the world can be used in British cash machines. Just look for your card issuer symbol on the machine. However, do bear in mind the fact that some cash machines charge a fee for withdrawal (about £1.50 per withdrawal). You'll be notified on screen before the withdrawal about any charges and you will have the option to cancel the transaction. Remember also that your own bank (in your own country) may charge you for card withdrawals.

Credit and debit cards

These are widely accepted across the UK. Almost all shops accept Visa and MasterCard – it is very rare to find a merchant that accepts one and does not accept the other. American Express, Diners, JCB, Maestro and Electron are also widely accepted. Discover Cards are not accepted in the UK. Some shops insist on a minimum transaction of £5 if you are paying by credit or debit card. Remember that you might be charged a foreign exchange transaction charge by your bank when using your card in the UK. Check with your bank before using your cards.

Some shops and supermarkets also offer a 'cash back' facility when you pay with a UK debit card. The minimum cash back is £10 and the maximum allowed is £50.

Most retailers now process payments using a 'Chip and Pin' facility. When paying for purchases your card is inserted into a verifying machine. Instead of signing you'll be asked enter your PIN number using the key pad. If your card does not have the Chip and PIN facility then you'll have to sign the receipt and hand it back to retailer.

POST OFFICE SERVICES

Post offices in the UK are generally open from 9.00am to 5.30pm, Monday to Friday, and 9.00am to 12 noon on Saturday. Some smaller post offices have their own operating hours and close early during the week. The standard cost for post within the UK is 30p for first class and 21p for second class, for a letter up to 60 grams. First class mail is quicker and is usually delivered the next day. Second class mail can take up to two or three days to reach its destination in the UK. Postcards or letters up to 20 grams to European Countries have a standard charge of 42p while for non-European countries postage is 47p for letters up to 10 grams. Special rates are available for printed matter or small packets. Check with your local post office before posting them. An Air Mail label is essential for all overseas letters. The post office also offers a Parcel Force service for sending parcels around the world. The cost of sending a parcel of up to 1kg within the UK is £3.60 by Parcel Force.

Important letters within the UK can be sent by recorded delivery, where a signature is obtained on delivery. This service is ideal when you need to prove that the items were received. You can use this service either first class or second class. There is standard fee of 66p on top of the postage.

Urgent letters within the UK can be sent by Special Delivery. This service guarantees delivery anywhere in the UK by 1pm the next day. The service costs £3.85 for a package up to 100 grams. For even more urgent letters, Special Delivery before 9am costs £7.95 for a letter up to 100 grams.

Urgent letters can be sent abroad by Swift Air. There is a standard fee of £3 (£5 for recorded) plus the standard air mail postage. Remember to fill in a CN22 customs declaration form if you are posting packages outside the European Union.

Stamps can be bought at many outlets including most newsagents, supermarkets and your students' union shops. A notice advertising the sale of stamps will be displayed on the shop window. Stamps can also be purchased from automatic stamp dispensers located in places such as supermarkets, shopping malls and train or bus stations. You can also buy and print stamps from the Royal Mail website (www.royalmail.co.uk).

The post office provides a range of other services, including:

- payment of TV licences

- payment of Vehicle Tax on cars and motorcycles

- payment of telephone, gas, electricity and water bills

- issuing and cashing of postal orders

- banking (selected banks only)

- a commission-free Bureau de Change

- International Money Transfer Service – Moneygram to send or receive money

- mail holding service

- redirection service when you move premises.

A Poste Restante service is also offered at all main post offices. You can receive mail anywhere in the UK at a main post office convenient to your location.

Post offices also offer other services including selling stationery and international telephone cards, fax facilities, film processing, and sending flowers or chocolates. Further details about Royal

Mail are available on the web at www.royalmail.co.uk or you can call their customer services on 0845 7950 950.

INSURANCE

It is important to insure your possessions against theft or loss. There are many low cost schemes available for students. Insurance agents will be able to advise you on the different policies available. Endsleigh Insurance (www.endsleigh.co.uk and 0800 028 3571) is recommended by the National Union of Students and has offices on most campuses. Your university or college may also run a scheme for students living in a hall of residence or private houses. Contact the university insurance office for further details. Most banks also offer possessions insurance policies for students who open a student account.

If you are planning to travel around Europe or elsewhere it is worth buying travel insurance for the duration of your trip. Travel insurance for a trip to Europe costs around £12 for ten days.

Car insurance is available from a wide number of insurance companies and is often cheaper if you buy it on the internet. Students should expect to pay around £350 for third party insurance. Some insurers offer a 'no claims' discount on motor insurance policies so it is worth bringing letters from your insurers in your country if you want a 'no claims' discount. Reputable insurers are:

- Direct Line (www.directline.com)
- Norwich Union (www.norwichunion.com)
- AXA (www.axa.com)

◆ Egg (www.egg.com).

UTILITIES

Water

It is safe to drink water directly from the tap unless there is a notice that says not to. Hard water problems exist in some regions in southern England. If you find that you don't like the taste of hard water you can buy a water filter from an appliance store. Water filters cost around £15.

Electricity

Electricity is supplied throughout the United Kingdom at 240V and 50Hz. Plugs have three square pins but adapters are widely available in electrical goods shops costing around £4.

SHOPPING

Supermarkets

There are several supermarkets in every town, selling a wide variety of foods. Smaller stores tend to be slightly more expensive than the supermarkets, but might be more convenient. Major supermarkets in the UK are Sainsbury's, Tesco, Asda, and Morrisons. Asda (a part of Walmart group) and Tesco are usually the cheapest, followed by Morrisons and Sainsbury's. Waitrose, part of the John Lewis partnership, is a little expensive but is reputed for its high quality products. Most towns also have specialist stores selling Indian, Italian, Arabic, Greek, Thai and Chinese food products. They can be found in the local *Yellow Pages*. Most supermarkets also offer the convenience of shopping online with a delivery service, sometimes free.

Pharmacies

Boots, Lloyds and Superdrug are popular high street pharmacies. They are usually open from 9.30am to 5.30pm Monday to Saturday and 10.00am to 4.00pm on Sundays. In addition to the high street pharmacies there are also several local pharmacies. Some towns also have a 24-hour pharmacy available – look in your local *Yellow Pages* for more details.

Alcohol

You can buy alcoholic drinks, to take away from off licences, such as Threshers, Winerack and Oddbins. There are also privately-run off licences in many towns. These are usually open from 9.00am to 10.00pm. Supermarkets offer the best prices however. The minimum age for buying alcohol in the UK is 18.

Department stores

Department stores are the focal point of shopping in almost every town in Britain. Major stores are John Lewis, House of Fraser, BHS and Debenhams. However, the heart of shopping in Britain is the high street where established brands and other consumer items are sold through a chain of shops. High streets are becoming very similar around the UK. You'll probably find the same kind of shops and goods wherever you are in the country.

Clothes

Clothes can be bought new from department and chain stores such as Gap, Next, John Lewis, House of Fraser, and Marks and Spencer. These can be found in shopping arcades in and around a town centre. Prices are generally more expensive during peak seasons, such as before Christmas, but are then heavily discounted during the New Year and summer sales.

Second-hand clothes can be bought from various charity shops such as Oxfam, Imperial Cancer Research and Age Concern. This is a cheap way of buying clothes and your money is given to charities. Second-hand clothes can also be bought very cheaply from jumble sales. You will find these advertised in your local paper.

Clothes/shoe sizes
Clothes and shoe sizes in the UK are different from continental European and American sizes. Most shops display European sizes alongside the standard UK sizes. Approximate conversions are given in the tables below.

Men's shirts

US/UK	14	14.5	15	15.5	16	16.5	17
Continental	36	37	38	39	40	41	42

Women's clothes

UK	8	10	12	14	16	18
US	6	8	10	12	14	16
Continental	36	38	40	42	44	46

Shoe sizes

UK	2	3	4	5	6	7	8	9	10	11	12	13
European	34	35.5	37	38.5	40	41	42	43	44.5	45.5	46.5	48
US (male)	3	4	5	6	7	8	9	10	11	12	13	14
US (female)	3.5	4.5	5.5	6.5	7.5	6.6	7.5	10.5	11.5	–	–	–

Electronic, electrical and computer goods

Dixons, Currys, Comet, Argos, Robert Dyas, House of Fraser and John Lewis are reputable dealers in electrical, electronic and computer goods. For second-hand goods, look around for adverts on your campus as graduate students tend to sell their goods at a low price when they finish their studies.

Bookstores

Waterstone's and Blackwells are major high street booksellers in the UK. You may find a branch on Campus. Books can also be purchased form WH Smith, John Menzies (in Scotland) and several second-hand bookshops in town. During term-time second-hand booksellers may also have a stall at the Students' Union selling academic and general books. Amazon.co.uk is also a popular online bookstore.

Look around for special deals during the New Year and summer sales. Shops are generally open from 9.00am to 5.30pm on weekdays (except Thursdays when some shops in large towns open until 8.00pm), from 9.00am to 6.00pm on Saturdays and from 11.00am to 17.00am on Sundays.

List of high street stores
Menswear: River Island, Next, Muji, French Connection, High and Mighty, TK Maxx, The Officers Club, Cirro Citterio, Burtons, Gap, Republic, Quicksilver, Zara, Primark, H&M, USC etc.

Womenswear: Miss Sixty, Muji, French Connection, Miss Selfridge, Warehouse, Principles, Monsoon, Next, River Island, Gap, Primark, H&M, USC, Dorothy Perkins, TK Maxx, Zara, Etam, Mango, Kookai, Oasis, etc.

Footwear: Clarks, Barratts, Schuh, Priceless, Jones, Ravel, Dune, High Rise, etc.

Sportswear: JJB Sports, JD Sports, etc.

Games/music/DVDs: HMV, Virgin, Oxfam, Fopp, Game, etc.

Other electronic/electric: Jessops, Robert Dyas, etc.

Jewellery: Goldsmiths, H. Samuel, Beaverbrooks, etc.

Toys/gadgets: The Entertainer, The Gadget Shop, Must Have It, etc.

Children's: Mamas and Papas, Mothercare, Early Learning Centre, etc.

Stationers: WH Smiths, Rymans, Clinton Cards etc.

Health and beauty: The Body Shop, Boots, Lush, The Perfume Shop, GNC, Holland and Barrett, etc.

Travel agents: STA Travel, Going Places, Thomas Cook, My Travel, Flight Centre, etc.

Others: The Pier, Crabtree and Evelyn, Natural World, Disney, Lawleys, Thorntons, etc.

Laundrettes

Laundrettes can be found all around town. The average cost of washing a load is around £3.00 (plus £1.00 for drying). Halls of residence usually have washing machines for student use and these are generally cheaper. You will need your own washing powder and fabric softener.

DISCOUNT CARDS

NUS (National Union of Students) cards
Issued free by your Students' Union an NUS card gives you discounts at most high street shops, museums, cinemas, restaurants, night clubs, bars, takeaways and other leisure activities. Further details about student discounts can be found online at www.nusonline.org.uk

ENTs (entertainments) card
This card it not worth having unless you are a serious clubber. Issued by your Students' Union the Ents card gives you discounts on entry prices to events in the Students' Union. The card costs around £10 and usually gives a pound off ticket prices to events in the Union.

Young Persons Railcard
This is worth having if you are planning to travel around the UK by train. It costs £20, is valid for a year and entitles you to a third off most rail fares throughout the UK. The railcard can be used by anyone under 26 years of age, or a student in full-time education. You can apply for one at your local student travel agency or directly at any train station. You'll need to take two photographs along with proof of your age (for example, your passport or Driver's Licence) or proof of your student status if you are older than 26 years. Check the website at www.youngpersons-railcard.co.uk for further details.

National Express Coach Card

This card gives you 30 per cent off coach travel run by National Express – a major coach operator in the UK – and its subsidiary Eurolines. The card costs £11 and is available from National Express offices or agents. To find out your nearest National Express agent call 08705 80 80 80 or look online to www.nationalexpress.com

International Student Identity Card (ISIC)

This is probably the only student card that is recognised across the world. An ISIC card gets you discounted flexible airline student tickets and other student discounts around the world. In the UK the card costs around £7 for a year and can be obtained from STA Travel branches or by mail order directly from ISIC. You'll need a photograph and proof of your student status. For further details see www.isiccard.com

Hostelling International Card (HIC)

Issued by the Youth Hostel Association, an HIC is useful when travelling around on a budget. Members are eligible for discounts on bed and breakfast in Youth Hostels around the world. Cards can be obtained from STA Travel branches around the country or at YHA hostels around the world. Check online at http://www.yha.org.uk for further details.

TIME

The standard time in the UK is Greenwich Mean Time or the Universal Time Co-ordinated (GMT/UTC) during summer. In March the clocks go forward one hour for British Summer Time. At the end of October the clocks go back one hour to Greenwich Mean Time.

Time difference

Argentina:	−3 hours	India:	+5½ hours
Australia (Canberra):	+10 hours	Japan:	+9 hours
Austria:	+1 hour	Kenya:	+3 hours
Brazil:	−3 hours	Malaysia:	+8 hours
Canada (Ottawa):	−5 hours	Saudi Arabia:	+3 hours
China:	+8 hours	South Africa:	+2 hours
France:	+1 hour	Taiwan:	+8 hours
Germany:	+1 hour	United States (Washington):	−5 hours
Greece:	+2 hours		

WEIGHTS AND MEASURES

Although the UK converted to metric coinage in the 1970s, you will find that many weights and measurements are still given using the imperial system. In shops and supermarkets you'll usually find both systems used. Distances are often still given in miles, fruits and vegetables may be sold in pounds and beer and milk are still sold in pints. A brief conversion table is given below.

Imperial	Metric
1 mile	1.6093 kilometre
1 inch	2.54 centimetre
1 pint	0.5683 litres
1 gallon (UK)	4.546 litres
1 pound	0.4536 kilograms
1 ounce	28.35 grams

TELEPHONE

The UK country code is +44. To dial another city/town in the UK you'll need to first enter the regional code and then the number. To dial an international number dial 00 then the country code, then the phone number. A list of regional and international dialling codes is given below.

National dialling codes

Aberdeen:	01224	Glasgow:	0141
Belfast:	02890	Leeds:	0113
Birmingham:	0121	Liverpool:	0151
Brighton:	01273	London:	0207 or 0208
Bristol:	0117	Manchester:	0161
Cambridge:	01223	Oxford:	01865
Cardiff:	02920	Sheffield:	0114
Edinburgh:	0131		

International dialling codes

Austria:	00 43	Ireland:	00 353
Belgium:	00 32	Italy:	00 39
Cyprus:	00 357	Netherlands:	00 31
Denmark:	00 45	Norway:	00 47
Finland:	00 358	Poland:	00 48
France:	00 33	Russian Federation:	00 7
Germany:	00 49	Spain:	00 34
Greece:	00 30	Sweden:	00 46

Other countries

Argentina:	00 54	Korea (South):	00 82
Brazil:	00 55	Malaysia:	00 60
Canada:	00 1	Mexico:	00 52
China:	00 86	Nigeria:	00 234
Ghana:	00 233	Saudi Arabia:	00 966
Hong Kong:	00 852	Singapore:	00 65
India:	00 91	South Africa:	00 27
Israel:	00 972	UAE:	00 971
Japan:	00 81	United States:	00 1
Kenya:	00 254		

Other useful numbers

100 – National operator (including reverse charges)
123 – Talking clock
150 – BT customer services
151 – Fault management
155 – International operator
999 – Emergency services

Public telephone boxes are operated by British Telecom (BT) and are either coin- or credit/debit card-operated. The minimum charge for making a call within the UK from a public call box is 30p for the first fifteen minutes and 10p for every fifteen minutes thereafter. Call charges are different for residential telephone lines. Call charges within the UK are cheaper between 6.00pm and 8.00am, and during weekends and bank holidays. For reverse charges dial 100 and ask the operator for a reverse charge call.

For international calls there are several other private telecommunication companies whose call charges may be lower than those of BT. You can buy their phone cards from newsagents, Students' Union shops and vending machines. International phone cards are available to the value of £5, £10 and £20. Check the charges of various cards to see which one is the cheapest to your country. When buying a phone card do remember to check whether there is a connection fee, daily maintenance fee or an expiry date.

Non-geographical and premium numbers
There are certain non-geographical and premium numbers that you need to be aware of. These are mainly used by businesses with a national presence and their numbers begin with 05, 08 or 09. Calls to non-geographical numbers can cost more than a

geographical number (one with the local area dialling code) and are charged at an even higher rate when calling from a mobile. Check with your service provider.

0800, 0808 or 0500:	Freephone numbers. Caller pays no charge when calling from a landline.
0845:	Local rate number. Caller pays a local rate from anywhere in the UK.
0844:	Flat rate of 5p a minute to call anywhere in the UK.
0870:	National rate numbers. Caller pays a variable national rate depending upon the time of the call.
0871:	Special rate number which costs 10p a minute.
0900:	Premium number that can cost up to £1.50 a minute.

Directory enquiries

Directory enquiry numbers in the UK begin with 118 followed by another three digits and are generally referred to as the '118 service'. There is no single directory enquiry number in the UK. There are more than 20 companies offering a directory enquiry service and the cost varies as they do not all charge at the same rate. Some companies charge a fixed fee for enquiries while others may charge by the minute, by a connection fee or simply limit the number of searches offered. Directory enquiry calls from your mobile phone are subject to additional charges by your service provider. Remember that the 118 service that offers you the best deal from your landline may not necessarily the best from your mobile.

The following is a summary of some of the directory enquiry numbers and their tariffs.

118 888	Calls cost 9p a minute plus an initial connection charge of 39p. Offers unlimited searches.
118 800	Calls cost 9p a minute plus an initial connection charge of 49p. Offers unlimited searches.
118 500	Calls cost 15p a minute plus an initial connection charge of 40p. Offers unlimited searches.
118 000	Calls cost 49p a minute and 20p thereafter. However, the number of searches is restricted to three only and calls are billed in 1 minute intervals.

Rates for international directory enquiries are different and are charged from around £1.50 per minute.

Free directory enquiries for personal or business numbers are available online at:

◆ www.bt.com
◆ www.yell.com
◆ www.thomsonlocal.com

Mobile phones

Britain has the largest number of mobile phones used *per capita* in Europe. Nearly 70 per cent of the population own a mobile phone. If you are in the UK for long enough, you might consider getting your own mobile phone. The five major established networks are O_2, Vodafone, Orange, T-Mobile and Three. Other service providers are Virgin Mobile, Easymobile and One Tel. Mobile phones in the UK are either on GSM or PCN networks. Phones from North Atlantic countries may not work in the UK unless they use a tri-band.

There are two main types of mobile phone tariffs in the UK – 'pay as you go' and a monthly rate. 'Pay as you go' phones cost from £25 (or £10 for a SIM card only). However, charges are expensive and calls cost around 25p a minute. You can top-up your phone credit over telephone or online using a credit/debit card, at most cash machines or by buying a top-up card. Top-up cards can be bought at newsagents, post offices, Students' Union shops and other local stores.

Mobiles with a monthly charge have cheaper call charges but you may find that you have to sign a contract with the phone company for at least a year. You will also have to produce proof of ID, proof of address in the UK and undergo a credit check before you are accepted. Three, Orange and T-Mobile are generally relaxed on their credit check rules and most overseas students get accepted by them. However, their coverage is limited and not as good as that of O_2 or Vodafone. Some companies may ask you for a deposit which is usually returned in three to six months.

You can find stores selling mobile phones in and all around town centres. Mobile phone companies have their own brand stores selling their phones. However, if you prefer an independent dealer then try one of the private shops on the high street. Carphone Warehouse is a reputable dealer that offers independent advice. The Link is another dealer that has plenty of branches in and around town. Other dealers are Phones4U and Mobile Phones Direct. Remember, it is a good idea to try to get a mobile phone on the same network that most of your friends use – calls between the same network are usually cheaper.

INTERNET

There are numerous cyber cafes around Britain that give you access to the internet for about £2–3 an hour with additional charges for printing or scanning. You can also access the internet at some of the BT phone boxes but these are expensive and cost around £1 for ten minutes.

Your university or college usually provides you with free internet access on site. You will be given a user name and password at the beginning of term. Free internet access is also available from local council libraries.

EMERGENCY SERVICES

The standard number for all emergencies in Britain is 999 (or 112 from a GSM phone). Calls to these numbers are free. You will then need to tell the operator which emergency service you require (ambulance, fire or police). You will be asked for your location and emergency details by the service. Assistance will then be despatched to you immediately.

Police

Police in the UK have a good reputation for maintaining law and order. The overall policing in the UK is divided into several regional police forces. Every regional police force has its own website which contains information and advice about police activities in the local area. You can find further details about police service in your area online at www.police.uk

PERSONAL SAFETY

Britain is generally a safe country. However, you should take certain precautions to keep yourself and your possessions safe. Keep valuable possessions with you or locked up in your room. Do not carry large sums of money on you or keep large sums in your room. Carry your money in an inside pocket or in a closed bag. It is wise to insure all your possessions so that you can replace them if they are lost or stolen. Remember that valuable jewellery, mobile phones and watches can be a target for theft if they are worn openly.

At bars and clubs avoid accepting drinks from strangers. There has recently been an increase in incidents in some bars where drinks are spiked. Avoid travelling alone at night. Try to travel with someone you know and keep to busy, well-lit and familiar areas (or take a taxi). If travelling by bus at night, sit near the driver. Avoid walking through subways or in dark deserted streets. Open areas such as parks or commons are not safe at night. During the day be alert to what is happening around you. As an extra precaution you can buy a personal alarm to carry for about £5.

RADIO

Popular national radio stations are BBC, Virgin, Kiss FM, Choice FM and Classic FM. BBC's Radio 1 (97.6–99.8Mhz) churns out music for the younger generation. The more popular, award-winning Radio 2 (88–91Mhz) plays a mix of music and current affairs that caters to a wider, mature taste; Radio 3's output (90.2–92.4Mhz) is mainly classical; Radio 4 (92.4–94.6Mhz) is a channel mainly dedicated to news, current affairs and drama. Radio 5 Live (693 and 909Khz) is generally a sports channel; Classic FM (100–

102Mhz) is a commercial station whose output, like Radio 3's, is classical music; and Virgin Radio (1215AM) is another popular commercial music channel. Besides the national radio stations, there are several local FM stations (at least two in every town) broadcasting current music and local news. A listing of radio programmes can be found in all Saturday and Sunday newspaper supplements and the *Radio Times* magazine.

You can also listen to most of the radio channels live over the internet at any time of day. Programmes are usually available on the website, for up to a week. DAB digital radios are becoming increasingly popular in the UK and currently cost from £50. With DAB digital radio you get far better reception and will be able to pause, rewind and record live radio programmes.

TELEVISION

There are five main national terrestrial channels (unless you want to pay extra for satellite, cable or digital TV). These are BBC1, BBC2, ITV1, Channel 4 and Channel 5. The popular channels are BBC1 and ITV1. BBC1 and BBC2 are public-funded channels and carry no advertisements. A few films are shown every night, but more are screened at the weekends. Channel 4 has many programmes that appeal to the British student audience. Channel 5 is relatively new and programmes are mainly American series.

Popular satellite and cable channels are Sky One, Sky Movies, Sky Sports, ITV2, Film Four, MTV, V channel, UK Gold and BBC Choice. A listing of television programmes can be found in all Saturday and Sunday newspaper supplements and the *Radio Times* magazine.

TV licence

It is compulsory to have a TV licence in the UK if you have a television (including PCs with TV cards). This is a unique way of funding BBC programmes. The cost of a licence for a colour TV is £126.50 and for a black and white set, £42.00. If you are to be in the UK for less than a year you might choose to pay by quarterly instalments. TV licences can be bought from your local post office or by telephoning the TV Licensing Authority on 0870 241 6468. Remember, you are liable for a heavy fine of up to £1,000 if you are caught using a TV without a licence. For more information check www.tvlicensing.co.uk

TV, video and DVD rentals

TVs, videos, and DVDs can be rented from rental shops around town. For example, the 'Box Clever' chain has shops in almost every town in the UK. The standard rental for a 21-inch TV is around £6 per week. However, you might find it cheaper to buy a second-hand TV.

Video tapes and DVDs can be rented from Blockbusters and several other local video rental companies. Blockbusters have many branches around town and have vending machines on some campuses. Rental for two nights costs around £3.50 for a new release. Your council library also rents music CDs, DVDs and videos at a slightly cheaper rate. Remember that videos in Britain operate on a PAL system. DVDs can also be rented online and cost from around £9.99 a month for unlimited rental.

NEWSPAPERS AND MAGAZINES

Newspapers

Newspapers in Britain cater for a wide variety of interests. The broadsheets report world news with commentary and analysis. Some broadsheets are also now printed in tabloid format. The tabloids generally present news in an eye-catching format and offer sensational stories. Among the serious national broadsheets, are the *Times* (owned by Rupert Murdoch), *The Daily Telegraph*, the *Guardian* and *The Independent*. The *Financial Times* is the paper for business news. Popular tabloid papers are *The Sun* (again owned by Rupert Murdoch), the *Daily Mail*, the *Daily Express*, the *Mirror,* and the *Daily Star*. Most regions have their own dailies, evening newspapers and a weekly newspaper providing local news. *The Yorkshire Post* and *Manchester Evening News* are popular in the North of England. In Scotland, there are three regional dailies: *The Scotsman, The Herald* and *The Aberdeen Press and Journal.*

Competition for readership among different newspapers is intensifying and their prices, as a consequence, are falling. Price of a typical national broadsheet paper is around 50p on weekdays and around £1.50 during weekends. Tabloids cost around 40p daily.

To boost circulation among students, most newspapers have cut their prices for students. During term-time newspapers in the Students' Union shops are sold for as little as 20p.

You can also buy foreign newspapers in the Students' Union shops and in most of the newsagents around town.

Magazines

Like newspapers, magazines in Britain cater for a wide variety of interests. Students can benefit from reduced subscription rates (up to 70 per cent) from the publishers. Check online at www.studentlife.com.uk for further details.

Maps

An A–Z street atlas of your town or city (published by A–Z Map Company) is useful to have. There are street atlases for almost all the major towns and cities in Britain and these cost around £4. They are a good source of reference to help you get around the town during your stay in the UK.

Ordnance Survey Land Ranger Series Maps are also full of information to help you to get to know your local area. The maps cost around £5 and show all the tourist information, footpaths, parks, camping sites, lakes and marshes, etc.

If you are planning to drive around Britain then it is worth getting a road atlas which costs about £5. Maps and atlases can be purchased from most Students' Union Shops, newsagents and bookshops.

EATING OUT

The UK was once ridiculed for its lack of variety in food, but the range of restaurants available has increased greatly in recent years. Today, you will find cuisines from almost every corner of the world. But remember if you are a student on a budget, eating out repeatedly can be very expensive.

Fish and chips is a traditional British meal that can be bought cheaply (from around £2.50). Harry Ramsden's is a renowned restaurant chain that specialises in upmarket fish and chips. The lower end of the market is dominated by burger chains (such as McDonalds, Burger King and KFC, where a meal costs around £3–4. There are also medium-priced restaurants that offer good Indian, Chinese, Italian, Thai and English cuisine.

There are numerous chains of restaurants that offer good value for money. These include pizzerias (like Pizza Express), traditional Chinese and Thai (like Yellow River Cafe) and family restaurants (like TGI Fridays, Beefeaters and Harvesters). You should expect to pay around £10–15 (more if you order alcohol) for a decent meal. Some restaurants offer 10–20 per cent student discounts on production of a valid NUS or Student card.

At the other end of the culinary spectrum is fine dining in elegant, gourmet restaurants where a three course meal can cost around £50–75. Vegetarians should not have a problem as most restaurants have a vegetarian menu or vegetarian options. There are usually a couple of vegetarian restaurants in every town and city. Many restaurants also serve Halal food.

ENTERTAINMENT

The core of student entertainment can be found at your Students' Union where a variety of events are held, from live bands to comedy to dance nights. Most students use the Students' Union because it is often less expensive (in terms of admission and alcohol prices) compared to bars and clubs in town. An events calendar is usually published at the beginning of every term.

Towns and cities have clubs offering diverse events during the week, although these can be expensive if they're not designated student nights. Clubs in town will have a stricter dress code and trainers and jeans are usually not allowed. The best way to find

out what's going on in your town is by looking in your local
newspapers, local entertainment guides and by keeping an eye out
for posters around your town and university campus.

Most towns now have a multiplex cinema screening the latest
movies. Almost all offer student discounts on production of a valid
student ID card. Odeon, UCI and Vue Cinemas are now found in
almost all university towns and cities in the UK. Independent
cinemas also operate around the UK screening films from around
the world. These are usually listed in the *Yellow Pages*.

The main focus of social life in Britain is the pub, where most
people meet to talk and drink. Pubs serve a wide variety of beers,
local ales, spirits, coffee, tea and food. Pubs are open from
11.00am to 11.00pm (Monday to Saturday) with last orders served
at 10.45pm. On Sundays pubs are open until 10.30pm.

Gay and lesbian life

Gay and lesbian life in Britain is diverse and vibrant. Universities
in Britain are very tolerant towards homosexuality and almost
every university has a Lesbian, Gay and Bisexual Society (LGB).
Check out their stalls during the freshers fair. Almost every town
has gay pubs, clubs, groups and community support. *Gay Times,
Boyz* and *Diva* are popular publications for the lesbian and gay
community and are available from newsagents. London,
Manchester, Brighton and Edinburgh have particularly vibrant
gay scenes.

Festivals and events in the UK

Throughout the year, a variety of exciting festivals and events take
place all around the UK. Some the events like Gay Pride and

Notting Hill Carnival are free, while others can cost up to £250. Some festival dates are listed below for 2006. further information can also be found online at www.efestivals.co.uk

Festivals and events in the UK
Cheltenham Folk Festival
10–12 February 2006
Cheltenham, Gloucestershire

Oxford Folk Festival
May 2006
Oxford

Isle of Wight Festival
9–11 June 2006
Newport, Isle of Wight

Wimbledon (Tennis)
26 June–9 July 2006
Wimbledon, London

Cambridge Folk Festival
July 2006
Cambridge, Cambridgeshire

Henley Regatta
28 June–2 July 2006
Henley-on-Thames, Oxfordshire

WOMAD (World Music and Dance)
July 2006
Reading, Berkshire

Edinburgh International Festival
13 August–2 September 2006
Edinburgh, Scotland

Edinburgh Festival Fringe
6–28 August 2006
Edinburgh, Scotland

Notting Hill Carnival
August 2006
Notting Hill, London

Hogmanay Celebrations
Friday 29 December 2005 until Monday 1 January 2006
Edinburgh

WEATHER

The weather is a favourite topic of conversation nationwide and
you will probably hear it mentioned several times a day. The
weather is very unpredictable – it can rain and be cold in summer
and there are sometimes pleasant days in winter. January and
February are usually the coldest months with temperatures falling
to zero and snowfall common in Scotland and Northern England.
In summer, temperatures can rise to 30°C. When you visit the
UK, come prepared for the changing weather patterns – some
warm clothes and an umbrella are essential.

RELIGION

Britain is predominantly Christian but most of the world's
religions are represented in the country. The two established
churches in Britain are the Anglican Church of England and the

Presbyterian Church of Scotland. The Monarch is the 'Supreme Governor' of the Church of England. However, not everyone participates in religion. According to a recent survey almost half of all adults in the UK expressed no religious affiliation.

Other religions in Britain are Hinduism, Judaism, Islam and Sikhism, Bahai Buddhism, Jainism and Zoroastrianism. Besides these, you'll also find followers of new religious movements, pagans and atheists.

BANK HOLIDAYS

Bank holidays are national (public) holidays in the UK. Bank holidays vary between England and Wales, Northern Ireland and Scotland. Most shops, restaurants and supermarkets are now open on bank holidays (although some for only a limited time).

Bank holidays for 2006

2	January:	New Year
17	March:	St Patrick's Day (Northern Ireland only)
14	April:	Good Friday
17	April:	Easter Monday
1	May:	May Day
29	May:	Spring Bank Holiday
12	July:	Battle of the Boyne (Northern Ireland only)
28	August:	August Bank Holiday
25	December:	Christmas
26	December:	Boxing Day

DRUGS

Use of all hallucinogenic drugs is strictly forbidden by law in the UK. Possession of and supply of drugs will result in a criminal conviction.

WEAPONS

Possession of weapons, including replica weapons, knives and CS spray is prohibited in the UK. Sentences are usually harsh and anyone found possessing a weapon can be jailed for a minimum of five years.

3

Travel

TRAVELLING TO THE UK

By air

The quickest way to get to the UK is by air. Major airports in the UK with good international connections are London Airports, Birmingham, Manchester, Edinburgh and Glasgow. You are likely to find cheap flights to London Airports. These have good train and bus connections to cities in the south of England. However, if the fares are reasonable then it might be quicker and cheaper to fly directly to the airport nearest to your university. This will save you the hassle of travelling by coach or train from major airports to your destination.

List of UK airports with airlines operating
Aberdeen: Air France, British Airways, Easyjet, KLM, Lufthansa, SAS.

Belfast: Aer Lingus, BMI, British Airways, Easyjet.

Birmingham: Aer Lingus, Air France, Air Malta, Air Slovakia, Alitalia, Bmibaby, BMI, British Airways, British European, Continental, Cyprus Airways, Czech Airlines, Emirates, First Choice Airways, Gulf Air, KLM, Lufthansa, MyTravel Lite, PIA, Ryanair, SAS-Scandinavian, Slovak Airlines, SN Brussels Airlines, Swiss, Turkmenistan, Uzbekistan Airways.

Bristol: Air France, British Airways, British European, Easyjet, KLM, Ryanair.

Cardiff: Aer Lingus, British Airways, KLM, Span Air, Tryolean.

East Midlands: BMI, British Airways, Lufthansa.

Edinburgh: Air France, BMI, British Airways, Easyjet, KLM, Lufthansa, Ryanair, SAS.

Glasgow: Air France, Continental, Easyjet, Emirates, Iceland Air, KLM, Lufthansa, Ryanair.

Leeds Bradford: Austrian, BMI, British European, KLM, Ryanair, Tyrolean.

Liverpool: Air Europa, BMI, Easyjet, Ryanair.

London (City): Aer Lingus, Air France, British European, KLM, Lufthansa, Sabena, Swiss.

London (Gatwick): Aer Lingus, Aeroflot, Afriqiyah Airways, Air Europa, Air France, Air Gabon, Air Malta, Air Seychelles, Air Transat, Air VIA Bulgarian Airways, Air Zimbabwe, Alitalia, American Trans Air, Antinea Airlines, Arkia, Azerbaijan Airlines, Balkan Bulgarian, BASE Airlines, Belavia, Braathens ASA, British Airways, Brymon, BWA, CSA Air, Cameroon Airlines, Continental, Croatia Airlines, Cubana, Cyprus Airways, Delta Air Lines, Easyjet, El Al, Emirates, Estonian Air, Etihad Airways, Finnair, First Choice Airways, FlyBE, Futura, Helvetic, Icelandic, Maersk Air.

London (Heathrow): Aer Lingus, Aeroflot, Aerolineas Argentinas, Air Algerie, Air Canada, Air China, Air France, Air India, Air Jamaica, Air Malta, Air Mauritius, Air Namibia, Air New Zealand, Alitalia, All Nippon Airways, American Airlines, Arkia, Austrian Airlines, Avianca, Balkan Bulgarian, Biman Bangladesh, British Airways, BWIA West Indies Airways, Cathay Pacific, Croatia Airlines, Cyprus Airways, Czech Airlines, Egyptair, El Al, Emirates, Ethiopian Airlines, EVA Air, Finnair, Gulf Air, Hellas, Iberia, Icelandair, Iran Air, Istanbul Airlines, Japan Airlines, Kenya Airways, KLM, PIA, Portugalia, Saudi Arabian, SN Brussels, Swiss, Syrian Arab, TAP Portugal, Turkish Airlines, United Airlines, Virgin Atlantic.

London (Luton): Easyjet, Monarch, Ryanair.

London (Stansted): Air Berlin, Basiq Air, CSA Czech Airlines, El Al, Germanwings, Iceland Express, Lux Air, Ryanair.

Manchester: Aer Lingus, Air Baltic, Air Canada, Air France, Air Jamaica, Air Malta, Alitalia, American Airlines, Austrian Airlines, British Airways, BWIA West Indies Airways, Cathay Pacific, China Airlines, Continental, Croatia Airlines, Cyprus Airways, Cyprus Turkish Airlines, Czech Airlines, Delta Air Lines, Emirates, Excel Airways, Finnair, First Choice Airways, FlyBE, Iberia, KLM, LOT, Lufthansa, Luxair, Malaysia Airlines, Monarch, MyTravel, Olympic, PIA, Qatar Airways, Ryanair, SAS-Scandinavian, Singapore Airlines, SN Brussels, Swiss, Syrian Arab.

Newcastle: Air France, BMI, British Airways, KLM, Lufthansa.

Norwich: KLM.

Southampton: Air Europa, Air France, BA, British European, Ryanair.

By train

Eurostar (www.eurostar.com or 08705 186 186) operates daily services between Paris, Lille, Brussels and London Waterloo. A journey from Paris to London takes around three hours, while a journey from Brussels to London takes around 3½ hours. Standard Fares for an APEX return are £49. Eurostar offers flexible student and youth fares. From London Waterloo there are excellent onward connections to Wales, South East England, and the Midlands.

By coach

EuroBus and Eurolines operate daily services to London Victoria Coach Station from 46 cities across Europe. From London Victoria there are excellent onward bus and train connections to other destinations around Britain. Fares are often as low as £30 for a return between Paris and London. However, the journey between London and Paris takes around ten hours, London and Frankfurt 19 hours and longer if you are travelling from an east European or Mediterranean country. Further details can be obtained online at www.eurolines.com or www.busabout.com.

Ferry

Regular ferry services operate between Dover and Calais; Folkestone and Boulogne; Portsmouth and Cherbourg or Le Havre; Plymouth and Santander; Newcastle and Stavanger or Bergen; Harwich and Esberj; Harwich and Hook of Holland; Harwich and Hamburg; Fishguard and Rosslare Europort; and Holyhead and Dublin or Dun Laoghaire. Ferries vary according to day and time of departure.

GETTING AROUND THE UK

Travel within Britain itself is relatively straightforward and there is a wide variety of options from cars and coaches to planes and trains.

Traveline

Traveline is a national travel information service offering impartial information on local buses, coaches and trains. You can contact them by phone on 0870 608 2 608 or online at www.traveline.org.uk

Cars

There is a vast network of roads in Britain, servicing all parts of the country. Further details on buying or hiring a car can be found on pages 70 and 71.

Hitchhiking is not very popular in the UK and not many motorists stop to pick up hitchhikers. You should avoid hitchhiking if you are travelling alone.

Trains

Probably the quickest way to travel around the UK is by train. Britain has an extensive network of trains. Although the fares are not cheap, train travel is a lot quicker than car or coach. Train services in the UK are operated by 25 different companies. Details of timetables, routes and fares can obtained from the National Rail helpline on 0845 7 48 49 50 or online at www.nationalrail. co.uk

Trains have two service classes: First and Standard. First Class tickets usually cost double the Standard Class. Long distance trains have buffet cars serving alcoholic drinks, refreshments and hot food. It is not necessary to book tickets in advance or to make a seat reservation unless you want the cheaper Super Advance or APEX tickets.

UK train fares are complex and can confuse even regular travellers. The most expensive tickets (without any restrictions) are *First Class*, followed by *Standard Open*. These tickets have no time or day restrictions. Saver fares are slightly cheaper, have restrictions and can generally be used at any time of day.

Super Saver fares are available on selected routes and can be used for travel only at off-peak times and days (usually Sunday to Thursday after 9.30am). There may be additional restrictions at Christmas or during other holiday seasons – check with National Rail before travelling.

Super Advance fares must be booked in advance (usually no later than 6.00pm on the day before the journey) and are limited in number. These tickets are valid on selected journeys only. The date and train details are shown on the ticket.

APEX fares are the cheapest but have a lot of restrictions. You'll need to book them at least seven days before your journey and like *Super Advance* they are valid for travel only on the date and train shown on the ticket. Seat reservations are compulsory for *Super Advance* and *APEX* tickets.

Buses

Travelling by bus or coach is the cheapest way to travel around Britain. The major coach operators in Britain are:

◆ National Express (www.nationalexpress.com or 08705 80 80 80)
◆ Stagecoach (www.stagecoachbus.com)
◆ Scottish Citylink (www.citylink.co.uk or 08705 50 50 50).

They link all the major cities and towns in the UK. All coaches in the UK are single class, non smoking, most have on-board toilets and some offer refreshment services. National Express offer unlimited travel passes to non-UK passport holders starting from £79 for seven days. You'll need to present your passport or ID card when buying your ticket. Megabus (www.megabus.com or 0900 160 0900) is another low-cost bus service that offers limited service around the UK. Similar to no frill airlines, Megabus prices start from £1 for a trip from Oxford to London.

Planes

The quickest way to travel around Britain is by air. Major airlines operating flights within the UK are:

* British Airways (www.ba.com or 0870 850 9850)
* British Midland International (www.flybmi.com or 0870 6007 555)
* British European (www.flybe.com or 0871 700 0535)
* Easyjet (www.easyjet.com)
* Ryanair (www.ryanair.com).

British Airways, the largest airline, offers a UK Airpass starting from £49 per trip. British Midland, the second largest scheduled airline, offers The Discover Europe Airpass, which can be used for scheduled flights in Britain and the rest of Europe. Both airlines serve almost all the major cities in the UK. These passes can be bought from STA Travel or other travel agents in the UK.

Ryanair and Easyjet are no frills airlines offering extremely low fares to destinations in the UK and Europe. Fares from London to Glasgow on Easyjet or Ryanair can start from as low as £1 (excluding taxes) each way. However, you should not expect certain levels of service (such as a free in-flight snack) from these airlines.

Driving

In the UK, vehicles are driven on the left-hand side of the road and anyone wanting to drive must have a valid licence. Driving regulations are contained in the *Highway Code* which can be bought in bookshops and petrol stations. The book costs around £2. You can also download it from the internet at www.highwaycode.gov.uk

Legally, you will only be able to use a foreign licence for the first 12 months of your stay, after which you must take a British driving test to obtain a British driving licence. Ask for form D100 at your post office for more information about how to get a licence, or download the form from the internet at www.dvla.gov.uk.

EEA nationals and nationals of the following countries are able to exchange their licence for a British Licence without taking a driving test: Australia, Barbados, British Virgin Islands, Canada, Hong Kong, Japan, Monaco, New Zealand, Singapore, South Korea, Switzerland and Zimbabwe.

You must be resident for at least six months in the UK before you can apply for a licence.

Learning to drive a car in the UK is very expensive and can cost around £1,500 (including lessons and test fees). There are plenty of driving schools in every town and their details are listed in *Yellow Pages*. Details about taking a driving test in the UK can be found online at www.dsa.gov.uk

Buying a car

A good place to look if you are planning to buy a second-hand car is the *Auto Trader* magazine or on the internet at www.autotrader.co.uk. *Auto Trader* has listings of cars and motorcycles in and near your area. *Exchange and Mart* is another magazine that advertises available cars in your area. To get an idea about what you should be paying for a second-hand car look at *Parkers Car Price Guide* (www.parkers.co.uk) which has listings of car prices according to their mileage and age.

Car advertisements can be found in your local newspapers and also on Students' Union notice-boards. Look around for as many cars as possible before buying. The Office of Fair Trading's booklet *Guide to Buying a Used Car* can also advise you on what to look for when buying a second-hand car. The booklet is available free of charge at your local council office or at your student advice centre. You can also find it on the internet at www.oft.gov.uk

By law, your car must be taxed, insured and have a Ministry of Transport (MOT) certificate. An MOT is a test of your vehicle's road-worthiness and is available at any approved MOT garage or centre. Tax discs are available from any post office and cost from about £100 per year depending upon your car engine-size. Leaflet V100 available at all post offices explains everything about registering, licensing, testing and insuring your vehicle. Vehicle insurance is available from a wide number of insurance companies. Further details about registering a car and driving a foreign registered car in the UK can be found online at www.dvla.gov.uk

Hiring a car

The main rental companies operating in the UK are:

- Avis (www.avis.co.uk or 0870 60 60 100).
- Hertz (www.hertz.co.uk or 08708 448844).
- Budget (www.budget.co.uk or 0870 156 56 56).
- Sixt (www.e-sixt.co.uk or 0870 156 75 67).
- National (www.national.co.uk or 0870 400 4502).
- Thrifty Car Rental (www.thrifty.co.uk or 01494 751 600).

You should expect to pay around £35 a day rental for a compact car on weekdays. Weekend rentals are cheaper and cost around £60 for a weekend (3 days). Easyrentacar (www.easyrentacar.com) based in London, Birmingham, Liverpool, Glasgow, Edinburgh and Manchester rents a compact car for as little as £6 per day.

Many rental companies don't hire to those under 23 or 25 years of age. Most car rental companies also require a credit card as a guarantee and some also insist on a valid EU licence. Before renting a car, check whether the price includes unlimited mileage, liability insurance and 24-hour roadside assistance. Some of the car rental companies offer a delivery and collection service to your door (for which there may be an extra charge). Several local companies also offer car rentals – check your local *Yellow Pages* for further information.

Bicycles

Bicycles are a popular transport option for students. New bicycles cost from around £100 up to £1,000, but second-hand bikes can be bought from £20 upwards. Halfords is one of the main dealers in new bicycles. For second-hand bikes look out for adverts in your local newspaper and on the Students' Union notice-boards. Second-hand bicycle shops are also listed in *Yellow Pages*.

If you buy a bike it is essential to buy a good lock, (preferably a D Lock) and to keep the bike locked at all times. Your local police can also stamp your bike with a security code so that if it is stolen it will be easily identifiable. It is also advisable to buy a bicycle helmet. Bike accidents are frequent and can result in serious head injuries. Helmets cost from around £16. Rules for cyclists can be found in the *Highway Code* which can be bought for around £2 in bookshops and petrol stations. You can also download it from the net at www.highwaycode.gov.uk

Taxis

Taxis are expensive in the UK and the rates vary around the country (with London and the South East being the most expensive). You should expect to pay around £5 for a short ride of less than a mile in London or other major cities in the South East. There are two types of taxi operating around the UK. Black cabs are licensed to pick up passengers in cities and towns. They have a standard meter inside and the fares are set by the local council. Up to five people can share these taxis.

Mini-cabs or private hire vehicles are normal cars with a Local Authority licence plate. They have to be pre-booked by telephone or at a local cab office. Check the fare before you travel as these taxis don't have a meter. Usually up to four people can share a mini cab although six to eight seater taxis are also available.

SAFETY TIPS FOR TAXIS

◆ Always use a licensed taxi or a private hire vehicle from a reputable licensed taxi hire firm.

◆ Make sure you only get into the car you ordered.

◆ Ask the cab firm for details of the car when you book (and give them your name).

◆ Make sure the driver knows what name the car was booked under.

◆ Before you get into a cab check that it has a Local Authority licence plate.

◆ Text the cab's number plate to a friend.

◆ Sit in the back of the taxi and do not give your personal details to the driver.

◆ If the driver is making you feel uneasy then ask him to stop in a busy public area and get out of the car.

Travel agencies

The only student travel agency currently available is STA Travel (www.statravel.co.uk or 08701 60 60 70). It has over 50 university and high street branches in the UK and specialises in selling discounted flight tickets, accommodation, visas, insurance, travel passes, European Rail tickets, and European overland tours for students and young people. The benefit of booking through STA Travel is the flexibility which many online sites and other travel agents do not offer. Most of the tickets purchased through STA Travel can be changed without any additional charges.

Other high street travel agents that offer competitive fares are Trailfinders (www.trailfinders.com), Flight Centre, Flight Bookers (www.ebookers.com), Thomas Cook (www.thomascook.co.uk), Going Places and First Choice. The travel sections of weekend papers also have listings of air fares and travel agents. Check their advertisements and phone around for the best prices. Before booking tickets or paying money do make sure that the travel agent is a member of ABTA (Association of British Travel Agents) or IATA (International Air Transport Association). These organisations offer protection if the travel agent or airline goes out of business.

Most of the airlines have now started selling student tickets directly through their websites. For example, KLM (www.klmuk.com) and Swiss Airlines (www.swiss.com) offer cheap fares to students travelling worldwide. Other online agents that offer competitive prices are:

- Expedia (www.expedia.co.uk)
- Travelocity (www.travelocity.co.uk)
- Opodo (www.opodo.co.uk)
- Ebookers (www.ebookers.com).

Immigration

TIP

Visa regulations are subject to change. You are advised to check the situation with your local British Embassy, high commission, foreign consulate or the Home Office before making any arrangements.

Now that you have been admitted to the university of your choice, you will need the British government to sanction your entry into the country. To encourage international students to study in the UK, the British government has streamlined the immigration regulations. However, you must still pay attention to the rules that are applicable to you.

International students no longer require work permits to enable them to work whilst studying in the UK. The introduction of the Highly Skilled Migrants Programme (HSMP) has permitted international students to work in the UK without a work permit after completing their course (see Chapter 10). Student visa applications at British missions abroad are now fast-tracked. A student applying for a visa or entry clearance or for an extension should experience only minimum difficulty in acquiring one.

PASSPORT OR TRAVEL DOCUMENTS

Your passport or travel documents should be valid for more than the duration of your studies in the UK. If they are about to expire, renew them before you apply for a visa or arrive in the UK. Citizens of the EEA (European Economic Area) do not necessarily need a valid passport and can use their National ID cards instead to travel to the UK.

Visa or entry clearance

Visa or entry clearance is an endorsement on your passport that allows you to enter a country for a specific purpose in a specific period of time.

EEA nationals

EEA nationals, including Swiss nationals, can enter and work in the UK freely without any restrictions. They need only to produce their valid passport or ID card at the port of entry.

EEA nations
Austria, Belgium, Cyprus, Czech Republic, Denmark, Estonia, Finland, France, Germany, Greece, Hungary, Iceland, Ireland, Italy, Latvia, Liechtenstein, Lithuania, Luxembourg, Malta, Netherlands, Norway, Poland, Portugal, Slovakia, Slovenia, Spain and Sweden.

Non-EEA nationals

Nationals from countries other than the ones mentioned on page 78 do not need a visa to come to the UK as a student for a course, the duration of which is less than six months. They will need to carry their proof of student status (letter of acceptance from the college or university) and proof of funding and accommodation while travelling to the UK. Upon checking these documents the immigration officer at the port of entry, will grant you permission to stay for the duration of the course. However, it is advisable to get an optional entry clearance as a student from your local British Embassy, High Commission or Consulate before leaving your country. This will make your clearance through immigration easier if you encounter any problems. An optional entry clearance will let you enter the UK temporarily and the opportunity to appeal if the immigration officer at the port of entry decides not to grant you permission to enter.

All non-EEA nationals (and their dependants) coming to the UK for a course lasting more than six months need to apply for an entry clearance at their country of residence before coming to the UK. It is no longer possible to obtain or to extend your visa or entry clearance at the port of entry.

Nationals from the following countries require a visa to enter the United Kingdom
Afghanistan, Albania, Angola, Armenia, Azerbaijan, Bahrain, Bangladesh, Belarus, Benin, Bhutan, Bosnia-Herzegovina, Bulgaria, Burkina Faso, Burma, Burundi, Cambodia, Cameroon, Cape Verde, Central African Republic, Chad, China, Colombia, Comoros, Congo, Cuba, Democratic Republic of Congo (Zaire), Djibouti, Dominican Republic, Ecuador, Egypt, Equatorial Guinea, Eritrea, Ethiopia, Fiji, Gabon, Gambia, Georgia, Ghana,

Guinea, Guinea Bissau, Guyana, Haiti, India, Indonesia, Iran, Iraq, Ivory Coast, Jamaica, Jordan, Kazakhstan, Kenya, Kyrgyzstan, Korea (North), Kuwait, Laos, Lebanon, Liberia, Libya, Macedonia, Madagascar, Mali, Mauritania, Moldova, Mongolia, Morocco, Mozambique, Nepal, Niger, Nigeria, Oman, Pakistan, Papua New Guinea, Peru, Philippines, Qatar, Romania, Russia, Rwanda, São Tomé e Principe, Saudi Arabia, Senegal, Sierra Leone, Somalia, Sri Lanka, Sudan, Surinam, Syria, Taiwan, Tajikistan, Tanzania, Thailand, Togo, Tunisia, Turkmenistan, Uganda, Ukraine, United Arab Emirates, Uzbekistan, Vietnam, Yemen, Zambia and Zimbabwe.

A stateless person or a person travelling on a non-national document rather than a passport is also required to have a visa before travelling to the UK.

HOW DO I APPLY FOR A STUDENT VISA OR ENTRY CLEARANCE?

You'll need to apply for student visa at the British Embassy, high commission or consulate in your country of residence well in advance of the start of your course. You'll need to fill in Non-Settlement Form VAF1 and submit it along with a passport-sized photograph and other supporting documents. Currently a student visa costs £85 to process irrespective of the length of stay. Forms and up-to-date guidance notes are provided free of charge by the UK missions abroad or can be downloaded from the internet at www.ukvisas.gov.uk

You will need to prove that you have been accepted onto a full-time course of study that involves a minimum of fifteen hours' study a week, at an educational institution recognised on the UK's

Department for Education and Skills (DfES) Register of Education and Training Providers (a letter of acceptance from your institution should be sufficient) and you will need confirmation of your accommodation (such as a letter from your university accommodation agency offering a place in a hall of residence). You will also need to prove that you can meet the course and living expenses (and those of your dependants) without working or claiming public funds (financial documents confirming your scholarship or bank statements confirming sufficient funds will prove this); that you meet the requirements of the course (degree certificates from your home country); and that you intend to leave the UK after you finish the course. You may be asked to attend an interview by the entry clearance officer to clarify certain matters in your application. British missions abroad may also ask residents in some countries to undergo a further medical examination. Student visa applications are usually processed within 24 hours (except in Nigeria, South Africa, Ethiopia, Thailand, Philippines and Pakistan, where the process can take up to 60 days).

Bringing in your dependants
You can bring your spouse and children under 18 years of age to the UK as long as you can prove that you are able to accommodate them and can financially support them without claiming public funds. The entry clearance or immigration officer will want to see your marriage certificate, a birth certificate for every child, and evidence of your student status as well as financial documents to prove that you'll be able to support your family in the UK. Your dependants will then be given permission to stay for the same duration as you. Dependants are permitted to work freely without a work permit as long as you stay for a minimum of 12 months.

Refusal and appeal

If you are refused a visa or entry clearance then the entry clearance officer has to give you written notice explaining why the application was refused. If you have a right to appeal, the entry clearance officer will give you two additional forms – a notice of appeal form (on which you can explain why you think he or she was wrong to refuse your application) and a leaflet explaining the appeals process. You will need to complete the notice of appeal form and return it within 28 days. The appeals process is free of charge.

Wrong type of visa or stamp

It rarely happens, but if you realise or feel that you have been given the wrong documentation contact your International Office or Student Advice Centre immediately. They can advise you on how to change your status. If you realise that you have applied for or been given the wrong visa or entry clearance then contact the British mission where you originally applied before you leave for the UK. Do *not* enter the UK with the wrong visa as it will cause severe problems.

ARRIVING IN THE UK

As soon as you arrive in the UK, you will have to go through passport control. There will be two queues, one for EEA and Swiss nationals and the other for non-EEA nationals. EEA and Swiss nationals need only to produce their passport or national ID card. For non-EEA nationals the immigration process is usually quick if you have a prior entry clearance, although you may still be questioned and asked to produce supporting documentation. You will also need to complete a landing card on which you'll be asked your full name, your nationality, date of

birth, profession and your address in the UK. If your
accommodation has not been confirmed, write your college or
university address. The immigration officer will then validate your
visa with a stamp on your passport confirming your entry to the
UK. Your visa is then valid until the date specified. The United
Kingdom Immigration Service at major ports of entry has a
telephone contact for general enquiries.

London (City)		020 7646 0088
London Gatwick	North Terminal:	01293 502 019
	South Terminal:	01293 567 282
London Heathrow	Terminal One:	020 8745 6809
	Terminal Two:	020 8745 6850
	Terminal Three:	020 8745 6900
	Terminal Four:	020 8745 4700
London Luton		01582 439 030
London Stansted		01279 680 118
London Waterloo Channel		
Rail Terminal		020 7919 5910
Birmingham Airport		0121 606 7350
Manchester Airport	Terminal One:	0161 489 2651
	Terminal Two:	0161 489 6230
Edinburgh		0131 348 4022
Glasgow		0141 848 5300
Dover Port		01304 200 400
Cardiff		01446 711580
Southampton		023 808 20140

Documents to carry when coming to the UK (for non-EEA nationals)

When travelling to the UK you will need to carry with you the
letter of acceptance from your university or college, proof of
funding, proof of accommodation (if it has been organised) and
your return air ticket (if your course is for less than six months).
If your spouse or children are travelling alone then they will also

need to carry, as well as the above, a photocopy of your passport and entry clearance. Try to arrive in the UK during office hours as this will enable you or the immigration officer to contact your university should a need arise.

When you arrive at a port in the UK

Arrivals
↓
Passport control
(EEA nationals or all other nationals)
(Non-EEA nationals will have to fill in a landing card,
show your passport and visa, letter from university or college
and proof of financial support)
↓
Health registration
(certain nationalities only)
↓
Baggage reclaim
↓
Customs
Green channel if you have nothing to declare
Blue channel for arrivals within EU
Red channel if you have something to declare
↓
Arrivals hall

Customs requirements and regulations

Customs allowance varies for travellers arriving from EU and non-EU Countries. Check the customs website at www.hmrc.gov.uk or with the British mission abroad before travelling. When entering a port you'll see three customs channels; take the green channel if you have nothing to declare, the blue channel if you are travelling from an EEA country or the red channel if you have something to declare. You are prohibited from bringing any of the following into the UK: drugs, explosives, firearms, offensive weapons, obscene publications and counterfeit currencies. You are also not permitted to bring in meat products from a non-EEA country.

Customs allowance
There are no limits imposed on goods from an EEA country. However, you may have to prove to a customs officer that the goods are for personal use only.

The following is a guide for people arriving from a non-EEA country only. For further information please check www.hmrc.gov.uk

Items	Limit
Cigarettes	200
Cigarillos	100
Tobacco	250 g
Spirits	1 litre
Fortified wine	2 litres
Wine	2 litres
Perfume	50 g
Eau de toilette	250 ml

POLICE REGISTRATION

Police registration is required for nationals if a requirement to register with the local police is endorsed or stamped on the visa or entry clearance or on the passport. By law, you should register with the police within seven days of arrival. You will need to take two passport-sized photographs, your passport and £35 to the front desk of your local police headquarters and register with them. The process is simple and takes approximately half an hour to complete. In most cases your university or college arranges for the local police to drop into the campus during the beginning of term to enable you to register on campus. Check with your university or college upon arrival.

Nationals of the following countries are required to register with the police within seven days of arrival in the UK

Afghanistan, Algeria, Argentina, Armenia, Azerbaijan, Bahrain, Belarus, Bolivia, Brazil, China, Colombia, Cuba, Egypt, Georgia, Iran, Iraq, Israel, Jordan, Kazakhstan, Kyrgyzstan, Kuwait, Lebanon, Libya, Moldova, Morocco, North Korea, Oman, Palestine, Peru, Qatar, Russia, Saudi Arabia, Sudan, Syria, Tajikistan, Tunisia, Turkey, Turkmenistan, United Arab Emirates, Ukraine, Uzbekistan and Yemen. A stateless person or a person travelling on a non-national document rather than a passport is also required to register with the police within seven days of arrival in the UK.

EXTENDING YOUR STUDENT VISA WHILST IN THE UK

You can extend your student visa by applying in person to the Home Office or by posting it to them one month before your current visa expires. The Home Office has now started charging a fee for this service. It costs £500 to apply in person at the public enquiry office (see below) or £250 for postal applications. You can extend your student visa four weeks before your current visa expires.

Forms

The Home Office has introduced a standard form (FLR) to be completed when applying for an extension of stay. These are available from your International Office or the Student Advice

Centre, who will also give advice on completing the form. Alternatively, you can obtain the form free of charge by calling the Home Office on 0870 241 0645 or by downloading it from the internet at www.ind.homeoffice.gov.uk

FLR (S) This form is for students who want to extend their stay in the UK as a student.

FLR (O) This form is for students who want to extend their stay in the UK as a short-term tourist after completing their course or to stay on until their graduation.

Before filling in the form read the guidance notes, make sure that you answer all the questions and submit the required supporting documentation. All supporting documents must be original.

Payment methods

Postal applications payment can be paid through a personal or business cheque, banker's draft, postal order, or a UK debit or credit card (Switch/Maestro, Delta, Solo, Electron, Visa, MasterCard or JCB only). Payments for an application lodged at the public enquiry office can be made through a personal cheque (accompanied by a cheque guarantee card up to the limit of the payment), banker's draft, postal order, a debit or credit card (Visa, MasterCard or JCB only). Cheques, banker's drafts and postal orders should be made payable to Home Office Leave to Remain.

Supporting documents

You will need to supply a letter from your university confirming acceptance to the course, details of your progress or attendance on your previous or current course, your last three months' UK bank statements and proof of funding or sponsorship.

Applying in person

If you need a decision urgently, you can apply in person at the Public Enquiry Offices (PEO) in Croydon (near London), Birmingham, Liverpool or Glasgow. You will need to make an appointment by calling the Public Enquiry Office for a reference number. You will then need to fill in the required application form and take it along with the fees and other supporting documents (your International Office or Student Advice Centre can verify these documents for you).

Your application will usually be processed and your passport stamped on the same day unless the officer decides that she or he requires further information (in which case you will be given a reference number and details of the documents required). You will need to make a payment of £500 either by postal order, credit or debit card, banker's draft or by cheque (with a cheque guarantee card for the total amount) before your application is processed. Do not take cash with you as it will not be accepted. The fee is non-refundable.

Croydon Public Enquiry Office
Immigration and Nationality Directorate
Lunar House
40 Wellesley Road
Croydon CR9 2BY
Tel: 0870 606 77 66
(Open Monday to Friday 9.00am to 4.00pm)

How to get there?

The train is the easiest and quickest way to get to the Croydon Public Enquiry Office. The nearest mainline station is East Croydon. Currently, the price of a standard day return ticket from London Victoria costs £6 or around £4 with a Young Persons Railcard. For up-to-date information on train times and fares contact National Rail Enquiries on 0845 7 48 49 50 or look online at www.nationalrail.co.uk

The PEO is situated on Wellesley Road. Upon arrival at East Croydon walk down George Street and turn right at the roundabout for Wellesley Road. Lunar House is the big multi-storey building on the right at the end of Wellesley Road.

Birmingham PEO will only accept applications from students in the West Midlands, Warwickshire, Staffordshire, Shropshire, Hereford and Worcestershire, East Midlands, Nottinghamshire, Derbyshire and Leicestershire.

There is no PEO in Northern Ireland. Students in Northern Ireland will either have to travel to Glasgow, Liverpool or to Croydon if they wish to make a personal application.

Glasgow Public Enquiry Office
Immigration and Nationality Directorate
Festival Court
200 Brand Street
Govan
Glasgow G51 1AR
Scotland
Tel: 0141 555 1258
(Open Monday to Friday 9.00am to 4.00pm)

How to get there?
The quickest and cheapest way to get to the Glasgow Public Enquiry Office is to take the SPT subway to Cessnock. Turn left as you come out of the station and walk 700 yards. Turn left again at the first junction and walk a further 700 yards on Brand Street. Festival Court is the building on the right hand side. A standard off-peak return ticket on the Glasgow underground costs £1.70. Frequent bus services also operate from Glasgow city centre and Union Street. Take bus No. 9 or No. 54 heading towards Paisley Wood West and get off at Govan.

Liverpool Public Enquiry Office
Immigration and Nationality Directorate
Reliance House
20 Water Street,
Liverpool
Tel: 0151 237 0405
(Open Monday to Friday 9.00am to 4.00pm)

How to get there?
The quickest and cheapest way to get there is by underground or by Merseyrail. The nearest underground station is James Street. Turn right as soon as you come out of the station and turn right again at the junction for the Strand. Go two blocks ahead for Water Street. Reliance House is right in the middle of Water Street opposite the Law Courts.

Public Enquiry Office
Immigration and Nationality Directorate
Dominion Court
41 Station Road

Solihull
Birmingham B91 3RT
Tel: 0121 704 5450
(Open Monday to Friday 9.00am to 4.00pm)

How to get there?
The nearest mainline station is Solihull. Birmingham PEO is
located on the station road which is five minutes' walk from
Solihull Station. To get there turn right as soon as you come out
of the station, go to the end of the station approach and turn left
for Station Road. An off-peak day return costs £2.50. Frequent
buses also operate from Birmingham city centre to Solihull town
centre. From Birmingham city centre take bus No. 37 or No. 57
heading towards Solihull town centre. The PEO is a short walk
from Solihull town centre bus stop.

Applying by post

Fill in the required application form and send it along with your
payment, passport and other supporting documents (your
international office or student advice centre will verify them for
you) by recorded delivery to the address given on the form. You
need to send the application form four weeks before your visa
expires. If you are unable to send all the supporting documents,
write a covering letter explaining why and details of when you will
be sending them. The Home Office usually allows one month for
you to send supporting documents. Keep a photocopy of your
application form and other supporting documents before you post
them.

Application timescale

It usually takes less than two to three weeks for your application
to be processed. Some applications may take longer if an

immigration officer needs more information before finalising the application. When an application comes under this category an acknowledgement will be sent and you should hear about the decision (or a request for supporting documents) within six weeks.

Applying through your university or college student batch scheme

The Immigration and Nationality Directorate has started accepting bulk student visa extension applications directly from universities and colleges. You can save the hassle of posting the application or queuing at the PEO by using this service. Check whether your university's International Office or your Student Advice Centre will do it for you. You'll need to fill in a standard application form, submit it along with payment, your passport and supporting documents (verified by the International Office or Student Advice Centre. Your Student Advice Centre or International Office will then send the application and supporting documents to the Home Office. You should have your passport back with your visa extension stamped within two to three weeks.

Refusal or late applications

Very rarely does a student's visa extension get rejected – unless the student has been found in breach of the immigration regulations. Contact your International Office or Student Advice Centre if your extension for stay has been refused. They will put you in touch with specialist bureaus who will then advise you on a further course of action.

Late applications get referred to a different department within the Home Office and might complicate your immigration status. If you are late in applying for your extension of stay contact your International Office or Student Advice Centre before you apply.

Immigration problems or queries

If you have any queries or problems on immigration matters contact your International Office or the Student Advice Centre. They have specialist advisers who will be able to assist you in the matter. It is a good idea to keep photocopies of all your important documents (passport, visa, and letters from the university or college) in a separate place in case of theft. You might want to leave a set of copies with your parents or friends in your country.

Immigration advice

Avoid taking private immigration advice from solicitors or agencies – you can get good immigration advice from your International Office or the Student Advice Centre free of charge. If they cannot advise you, they will refer you to a specialist immigration advisory service in your local area. You can also obtain independent advice and help from specialist immigration advisory services or your local Citizens Advice Bureau free of charge. If seeking private immigration advice, then do verify whether the agency is qualified and registered with the Office of Immigration Services Commissioner (OISC).

Immigration Advisory Service (IAS)

The IAS is a voluntary organisation, independent of the government, which provides free and confidential immigration advice free of charge.

Immigration Advisory Service
3rd Floor
County House
190 Great Dover Street
London SE1 4YB
Tel: 020 7967 1200. Duty office: 020 8814 1559
Fax: 020 7403 5875
email: advice@iasuk.org
http://www.ias.org.uk

The IAS also has local offices in Birmingham, Cardiff, Gatwick
Airport, Glasgow, Harmondsworth, Heathrow Airport, Leeds and
Manchester.

UKCOSA
The United Kingdom Council for Overseas Student Affairs offers
a free confidential telephone advice line to overseas students on
immigration matters. The advice line is open from 1.00pm to
4.00pm, Monday to Friday.

UKCOSA
9–17 St Albans Place
London N1 ONX
Tel: 020 7288 4330
Fax: 020 7288 4360
http://www.ukcosa.org.uk

JCWI
The Joint Council for the Welfare of Immigrants is another
voluntary organisation that provides free immigration advice.
They offer a confidential telephone advice line.

The Joint Council for the Welfare of Immigrants
115 Old Street
London EC1V 9RT
Tel: 020 7251 8708

VISAS TO EUROPEAN (SCHENGEN) COUNTRIES

What is a Schengen visa?

A Schengen visa is a unified visa that is issued by countries that are active members of the Schengen agreement. These are Austria, Belgium, Denmark, Finland, France, Germany, Greece, Iceland, Italy, Luxembourg, Norway, the Netherlands, Spain, Sweden and Portugal. The agreement has abolished internal border controls and allows free movement of people within the Schengen area of the member states. A Schengen visa issued by a member state is valid for the territory of all member states. Britain is not a member of Schengen Agreement.

Do I need a Schengen visa to travel around Europe?

Nationals from the following countries do not usually need a visa to enter Schengen territory: Andorra, Argentina, Australia, Bermuda, Bolivia, Brazil, Brunei, Bulgaria, Canada, Chile, Costa Rica, Ecuador, El Salvador, Guatemala, Honduras, Hong Kong, Hungary, Israel, Japan, South Korea, Macao, Malaysia, Mexico, Monaco, New Zealand, Nicaragua, Panama, Paraguay, Romania, San Marino, Singapore, Uruguay, USA and Venezuela.

This list varies between the Schengen countries and is subject to change. Some Schengen countries also impose temporary restrictions on free travel and close the border occasionally. Check with the embassy or consulate before travelling.

Visas to Europe are fairly easy to get for students in the UK with France and Germany being very lenient in their issue and generous with duration. Both the French and German Consulates are known to issue multiple-entry Schengen visas for three to six months' duration. Visas to new EU member states are more difficult to obtain.

Where to apply for a Schengen visa

You need to apply for a visa at the embassy or consulate of the Schengen country that is the country of your main destination. According to Schengen regulations, the country of main destination is the country where you will spend the longest part of your stay in the Schengen area. If you are not certain of your main destination, then you can apply for your visa at the Consulate of the country of first entry in the Schengen area. If unsure about the above, then check with your International Office or your Student Advice Centre.

How to apply for a Schengen visa

Applying in person
All applicants who wish to visit Schengen countries, except Sweden, must book an appointment with the consulate before applying for a visa. Appointments can either be booked by phone or via the internet. Sweden operates a first-come-first-served basis and around 50 tokens are issued by the consulate in London every morning.

Appointments by phone
You can book an appointment with the embassy or consulate by dialling a special automated appointment booking line at least one month before your planned journey. The call costs £1.00 per

minute and usually lasts for around 10 minutes. You'll then have
to choose the date and the time for your visit to the embassy or
consulate. The system will record your passport number and your
address. An appointment letter will then be sent to your address
which you need to take with you to the embassy or consulate on
the day of your appointment. Appointments can be booked for up
to four persons travelling together.

Appointments by internet or email

The French Consulate now offer booking via the internet, while
the Austrian Consulate lets you book an appointment by email.
You will need to give your passport details, dates of your trip and
your UK visa details. A letter will then be sent to you either as an
email attachment or by post. You'll need to take that with you
when you go to the embassy for your interview.

Applying by post

Some consulates permit residents living away from Greater
London to post their application. The distance varies with each
individual consulate. The requirements are the same. You'll need
to send all the supporting documents and payment (cheque, postal
order or banker's draft only) along with a completed application
form. Make sure you post your application by recorded delivery
and remember to enclose a pre-paid recorded delivery envelope for
the safe return of your passport.

Visa service

Visa services exist all around Britain and you can find them listed
in local newspapers, magazines and your local *Yellow Pages*. They
offer assistance in submitting and collecting your application from
the embassy for a fee. You may find it convenient to use this
service because it avoids you having to queue at the embassy or

consulate which will save you time. You'll need to fill in the required application form and hand it over to the visa service along with your supporting documents and fees. The visa service will then hand over your application to the embassy/consulate. The cost varies from company to company with some charging additional fees of up to £20 per hour for queuing. Usually companies in London charge around £80 plus the visa fee. If everything is in order, the passport, along with the endorsed visa is returned within 24 hours. No special favours are shown to applications submitted through a visa service company. Embassies and consulates treat all applications the same. Popular ones are Visaservice (Tel: 0870 890 0185, www.visaservice.co.uk), and the Schengen Office (Tel: 020 7240 3535, www.theschengenoffice.com).

Schengen visa requirements
Visa requirements vary according to embassies and consulates with most of them insisting on seeing proof of your student status, sufficient funds to cover your trip (around £35–£40 per day), travel insurance, a return ticket to your country of residence and proof of accommodation (hotel or hostel reservation) in the country you are visiting. If you are staying with friends, then you need to submit an original Certificate of Board and Lodging. This must be obtained from the local town hall or police station by your friends in the Schengen country.

You'll also need to submit two passport-size photographs along with your application. The processing time varies anything from a day to a month depending upon your nationality. The cost of a Schengen visa varies from £6–35 depending upon the consulate you apply to. Some embassies and consulates accept cheques and credit cards, however, it is best to check their website before you go. Visa fees are also subject to change every month depending on the exchange rate between the euro and pound. All visa fees are non refundable.

Make sure that your passport is valid for more than six months. Some embassies and consulates are known to insist that your 'leave to remain in UK' is valid for more than three months before your date of travel. You can download application forms from the respective embassy websites.

When to apply
You should apply well in advance – usually a month and a half before you intend to travel. Appointments get quickly booked up during the months of March, June, July, August and, in particular, December.

Schengen countries embassies and consulates in London
Austrian Embassy
18 Belgrave Mews West
London SW1X 8HU
Tel: 020 7235 3731
Fax: 020 7344 0292
24-hour visa information number: 09065 508 961
Visa booking number: 020 7344 3289
www.austria.org.uk
Email: visa@austria.org.uk
Nearest tube station: Hyde Park Corner

Belgian Embassy
103–105 Eaton Square
London SW1W 9AB
Tel: 020 7470 3700
Fax: 020 7470 3710
24-hour visa information number: 09065 508 963
Visa booking number: 09065 540 777
www.diplobel.org/uk
Email: belconsul@aol.com
Nearest tube station: Victoria

Danish Embassy
(Also issues visas for Iceland)
55 Sloane Street
London SW1
Tel: 020 7235 9531
Fax: 020 8333 0266
24-hour visa information number: 09065 508 975
Visa booking number: 09065 540 755
www.denmark.org.uk
Email: lonamb@um.dk
Nearest tube station: Knightsbridge

Finnish Embassy
38 Chesham Place
London SW1
Tel: 020 7235 9531
Fax: 020 7235 3680
24-hour visa information number: 09065 508 1122
www.finemb.org.uk

Email: sanomat.lon@formin.fi
Nearest tube station: Hyde Park Corner

French Consulate
6A Cromwell Place
London SW7
Tel: 020 7838 2000
Fax: 09001 669932
24-hour visa information number: 09065 508 940
www.ambafrance.org.uk
Nearest tube station: South Kensington

German Embassy
23 Belgrave Square
London SW1
Tel: 020 7824 1300
Fax: 020 7824 1449
www.german-embassy.org.uk
24-hour visa information number: 09065 508 922
Visa booking number: 09065 540 740
Nearest tube station: Hyde Park Corner

Greek Embassy
1A Holland Park
London W11 3TP
Tel: 020 7221 6467
Fax: 020 7824 1449
24-hour visa information number: 0906 550 8983
Visa booking number: 09065 540 744.
www.greekembassy.org.uk

Email: consulategeneral@greekembassy.org.uk
Nearest tube stations: Hyde Park Corner or Knightsbridge

Italian Consulate
38 Eaton Place
London SW1X 8AN
Tel: 020 7235 9371
Fax: 020 7823 1609
24-hour visa information number: 09065 508 984#
Visa booking number: 09065 540 707
www.embitaly.org.uk
Email: visti.londra@esteri.it
Nearest tube station: Victoria

Luxembourg Embassy
27 Wilton Crescent
London SW1X 8SD
Tel: 020 7235 6961
Fax: 020 7235 6961
www.luxembourg.co.uk
Email: embassy@luxembourg.co.uk
Nearest tube station: Hyde Park Corner

The Netherlands Embassy
38 Hyde Park Gate
London SW7 5DP
Tel: 020 7590 3200
Fax: 020 7225 0947
24-hour visa information number: 09065 508 916
Visa booking number: 09065 540 720

www.netherlands-embassy.org.uk
Email: consular@netherlands-embassy.org.uk
Nearest tube station: Gloucester Road

Norwegian Embassy
25 Belgrave Square
London SW1X 8QD
Tel: 020 7591 5500
Fax: 020 7245 6993
www.norway.org.uk
Email: emb.London@mfa.no
Nearest tube station: Hyde Park Corner

Portuguese Embassy
3 Portland Place
London
W1N 3AA
Tel: 0870 005 6970 or 020 7581 8722
Fax: 020 7581 3085
24-hour visa information number: 09065 508 948
Email: portembassy-london@dailin.net
Nearest tube station: Knightsbridge

Spanish Embassy
20 Draycott Place
London SW3 2RZ
Tel: 020 7589 8989
Fax: 020 7581 7888
24-hour visa information number: 0906 508 970
Email: embespuk@mail.mae.es

Swedish Embassy
11 Montague Place
London W1H 2AL
Tel: 020 7917 6413
Fax: 020 7917 6400
24-hour visa information number: 020 7917 6400
www.swedish-embassy.org.uk
Email: ambassaden.london-visum@foreign.ministry.se
Nearest tube station: Goodge Street

Students in Scotland
Students living in Scotland can also apply directly with the
consulates in Edinburgh in person or by post. Not all Schengen
countries have consulates in Scotland. Consulates are open from
09.00am to 12.00 noon, Monday to Friday. Please call them to
check whether they will deal with your application.

The Danish Consulate
4 Royal Terrace
Edinburgh
Midlothian EH7 5AB
Tel: 0131 556 4263

French Consulate General
11 Randolph Crescent
Edinburgh
Midlothian EH3 7TT
Tel: 0131 225 7954

German Consulate
16 Eglinton Crescent
Edinburgh
Midlothian EH12 5DG
Tel: 0131 337 2323

Italian Consulate General
32 Melville Street
Edinburgh
Midlothian EH 3 7PG
Tel: 0131 226 3631

Netherlands Consulate
53 George Street
Edinburgh
Midlothian EH 2 2HT
Tel: 0131 220 3226

The Norwegian Consulate
86 George Street
Edinburgh
Midlothian EH2 3BU
Tel: 0131 226 5701

Spanish Consulate General
63 North Castle Street
Edinburgh
Midlothian EH2 3LJ
Tel: 0131 220 1843

Visas to Switzerland

Switzerland has recently relaxed its visa regulations in order to boost its tourist industry. Nationals from the following countries do not need a visa to travel to Switzerland for a visit: EEA member states, Andorra, Australia, Brunei, Fiji, Hong Kong, Israel, Japan, Kiribati, Malaysia, Monaco, New Zealand, San Marino, Singapore, Solomon Islands, South Africa, South Korea, Tuvalu and all North, Central and South American countries including those in the West Indies (Caribbean Islands) with the exception of: Belize, Bolivia, Colombia, Cuba, Dominican Republic, Ecuador, Haiti and Peru whose nationals need a visa.

All other nationals who hold a Residence Permit for the UK endorsed on the passport do not require a visa to travel to Switzerland for up to three months. A UK residence permit or a UK temporary residence permit (one usually given to students) has to be originally issued for more than six months and one day. At the time of entry into Switzerland this permit must be valid for a further three months and the passport must be valid for three months after the date of departure from Switzerland. Check with the Swiss embassy before travelling.

Swiss Embassy
16 Montague Place
London W1H 2BQ
Tel: 020 7616 6000
www.swissembassy.org.uk
Nearest tube station: Baker Street

VISAS TO OTHER EUROPEAN UNION COUNTRIES

Do I need a visa?

EEA nationals do not need a visa to travel around the other EU member states. Nationals of Andorra, Argentina, Australia, Bermuda, Bolivia, Brazil, Brunei, Bulgaria, Canada, Chile, Costa Rica, Ecuador, El Salvador, Guatemala, Honduras, Hong Kong, Hungary, Israel, Japan, Macao, Malaysia, Mexico, Monaco, New Zealand, Nicaragua, Panama, Paraguay, Romania, San Marino, Singapore, South Korea, Uruguay, USA and Venezuela do not require visas to visit most of the new EU member states.

Visa requirements

Visa requirements to other European countries are similar to Schengen visa requirements with most of them insisting on seeing proof of your student status, sufficient funds to cover your trip, travel insurance, a return ticket to your country of residence, an invitation letter and proof of accommodation in the country you are visiting. Processing times vary for some nationalities with countries like Latvia and Slovakia insisting on obtaining a clearance from their home ministry before issuing a visa. At the moment, there is no need to book an appointment and visas are issued on a first-come-first-served basis. Fees vary according to the type and the duration of the visa.

Cyprus
Cyprus High Commission
93 Park Street
London W1K 7ET
Tel: 020 7240 2488
Fax: 020 7836 2602

cyprus.embassyhomepage.com*
Nearest tube station: Canon Street

Czech Republic
Embassy of the Czech Republic
26 Kensington Palace Gardens
London W8 4QY
Tel: 020 7243 1115
24-hour visa information number: 09069 101060
Fax: 020 7243 7926
www.czechembassy.org.uk
Nearest tube station: Notting Hill Gate

Estonia
Embassy of Estonia
16 Hyde Park Gate
London SW7 5DG
Tel: 020 7589 3428
www.estonia.gov.uk
Nearest tube station: Hyde Park Corner

Hungary
Hungarian Embassy
35B Eaton Place
London SW1X 8BY
Tel: 020 7235 2664
Fax: 020 7235 8630
www.huemblon.org.uk
Nearest tube station: Victoria

Ireland
Irish Embassy
17 Grosvenor Place
London SW1X 7HR
Tel: 020 7235 2171
ireland.embassyhomepage.com*
Nearest tube station: Hyde Park Corner

Latvia
Embassy of Latvia
45 Nottingham Place
London W1M 3FE
Tel: 020 7312 0040
Fax: 020 7312 0042
latvia.embassyhomepage.com*
Nearest tube station: Baker Street

Lithuania
Lithuanian Embassy
84 Gloucester Place
London W1U 6AU
Tel: 020 7486 6401/2
Fax: 020 7486 6403
lithuania.embassyhomepage.com*
Nearest tube station: Baker Street

Malta
High Commission of Malta
Malta House
36–38 Piccadilly
London W1V 0PP
Tel: 020 7292 4800

Fax: 020 7734 1831
malta.embassyhomepage.com*
Nearest tube station: Piccadilly Circus

Poland
Polish Consulate
73 New Cavendish Street
London W1W 6LS
Tel: 0870 774 2800
www.polishembassy.org.uk
Nearest tube station: Great Portland Street

Slovakia
Slovak Embassy
25 Kensington Palace Gardens
London W8 4QY
Tel: 020 7313 6470/7243 0803
Fax: 020 7313 6481
www.slovakembassy.co.uk
Nearest tube station: Notting Hill Gate

Slovenia
Embassy of the Republic of Slovenia
10 Little College Street
London SW1P 3SH
Tel: 020 7222 5400
Fax: 020 7222 5277
slovenia.embassyhomepage.com*
Nearest tube station: Westminster

* Embassyhomepage.com is privately run and is not an official website of the embassy, high commission or consulate.

CONTACTING YOUR EMBASSY FOR HELP

Most countries have diplomatic representation in the UK. You might have to register with your embassy depending on your national requirements. It is useful to have the contact details of your embassy in case of any trouble. The following are contact details of a few of the diplomatic representations in the UK. Full embassy listings are available on the web at www.fco.gov.uk

American Embassy
24 Grosvenor Square
London W1A 2LH
Tel: 020 7499 9000
Fax: 020 7408 8020
www.usembassy.org.uk
Nearest tube station: Bond Street

Australia High Commission
Australia House
Strand
London WC2B 4LA
Tel: 020 7379 4334
Fax: 0207 240 5333
www.australia.org.uk
Nearest tube station: Temple

Brazilian Embassy
32 Green Street
London W1K 7AT
Tel: 020 7499 0877
Fax: 020 7399 0877

www.brazil.org.uk
Nearest tube station: Marble Arch

Canadian High Commission
38 Grosvenor Street
London W1K 4AA
Tel: 020 7258 6600
Fax: 020 7258 6333
www.canada.org.uk
Nearest tube station: Bond Street

Embassy of the People's Republic of China
49–51 Portland Place
London W1B 4JL
Tel: 020 7631 1430
Fax: 020 7433 3 653
www.chinese-embassy.org.uk
Nearest tube station: Regents Park

Ghana High Commission
13 Belgrave Square
London SW1X 8PN
Tel: 020 7235 4142
Fax: 020 7245 9552
www.ghana-com.co.uk
Nearest tube station: Gloucester Road

Indian High Commission
India House
Aldwych

London WC2B 4NA
Tel: 020 7836 8484
Fax: 020 7836 4331
www.hcilondon.org
Nearest tube station: Holborn

Jamaica High Commission
1–2 Prince Consort Road
London SW7 2BZ
Tel: 020 7823 9911
Fax: 020 7589 5154
www.jhcuk.com
Nearest tube station: Gloucester Road

Embassy of Japan
101–104 Piccadilly
London W1J 7J
Tel: 020 7465 6500
Fax: 020 7491 9348
www.uk.emb-japan.go.jp
Nearest tube station: Green Park

Kenya High Commission
45 Portland Place
London W1N 4AS
Tel: 020 7636 2371
Fax: 020 7323 6717
www.kenyahighcommission.com
Nearest tube station: Oxford Circus

Embassy of the Republic of Korea
60 Buckingham Gate
London SW1 6AJ
Tel: 020 7227 5500
Fax: 020 7227 5503
korea.embassyhomepage.com*
Nearest tube station: High Street Kensington

Malaysia High Commission
45 Belgrave Square
London SW1X 8QT
Tel: 0207 235 8033
Fax: 0207 937 2925
malaysia.embassyhomepage.com*
Nearest tube station: Knightsbridge

Mexican Embassy
42 Hertford Street
London W1J 7JR
Tel: 020 7499 8586
Fax: 020 7495 4035
www.mexicanconsulate.org.uk
Nearest tube station: Hyde Park

Nigeria High Commission
9 Northumberland Avenue
London WC2N 5BX
Tel: 020 7839 1244
Fax: 020 7839 8746
www.nigeriahc.org.uk
Nearest tube station: Charing Cross

Pakistan Embassy
35–36 Lowndes Square
London SW1X 9JN
Tel: 020 7644 9200
Fax: 020 7644 9224
www.pakmission-uk.gov.pk
Nearest tube station: Knightsbridge

Russian Embassy
6 Kensington Palace Gardens
London W8 4QX
Tel: 020 7229 2666
Fax: 020 7727 8625
www.rustradeuk.org
Nearest tube station: High Street Kensington

South Africa High Commission
South Africa House
Trafalgar Square
London WC2 5DP
Tel: 020 7451 729
Fax: 020 7451 7284
www.southafricahouse.com
Nearest tube station: Charing Cross

Singapore High Commission
9 Wilton Crescent
London SW1X 8SP
Tel: 020 7235 8315
Fax: 0207 245 6583

www.mfa.gov.sg/london/
Nearest tube station: Hyde Park Corner

Saudi Arabia Embassy
30 Charles Street
London W1J 5DZ
Tel: 020 7917 3000
Fax: 020 7917 3255
www.saudiembassy.org.uk
Nearest tube station: Green Park

Sri Lanka High Commission
13 Hyde Park Gardens
London W2 2LU
Tel: 020 7262 1841
Fax: 020 7262 7970
www.slhclondon.org
Nearest tube station: Lancaster Gate

Taipei Representative Office
50 Grosvenor Gardens
London SW1W 0EB
Tel: 020 7396 9152
Fax: 020 7600 315
www.roc-taiwan.org.uk
Nearest tube station: Victoria

Tanzania High Commission
43 Hertford Street
London W1C 1AS

Tel: 020 7569 1470
Fax: 020 7495 8817
www.tanzania-online.gov.uk
Nearest tube station: Hyde Park Corner

Thailand Embassy
28 Princess Gate
London SW7 5JB
Tel: 020 7589 2944
Fax: 020 7823 9695
Nearest tube station: Gloucester Road

High Commission of Uganda
58–59 Trafalgar Square
London WC2N 5DX
Tel: 020 7839 5783
Fax: 020 7839 8925
Nearest tube station: Charing Cross

Ukraine Embassy
60 Holland Park
London W11 3SJ
Tel: 020 7727 6312
Fax: 020 7792 1708
www.ukremb.org.uk
Nearest tube station: Notting Hill Gate

Health

One of the biggest fears about any prospective long stay in a foreign country is health. People from tropical countries worry what it would be like to stay in a country that has a colder climate, and fear that this could lead to contracting the common cold. The doctor–patient relationship is a source of concern too, as this is also different in each country. Medical expenses that could take a big chunk of a student's shoestring budget are another common worry, as are some highly publicised diseases that the UK has been associated with (namely BSE or Mad Cow Disease) or sexual morality leading to the possible spread of sexual diseases. Finally the prevalence of mental illnesses, the effect of these on others, and the availability and misuse of drugs to cure them, are a point of concern to some people.

Rest assured, the UK is a healthy place and the government exercises considerable vigilance against the outbreak of disease. If you exercise elementary precautions, you can lead a normal, healthy life. It is necessary, however, for students to understand the health system of the UK in order to get the best possible medical care when they need it.

You are unlikely to get anything more serious than a cold or flu. However, do bear in mind that you will be living in a different climate, eating a different diet, and be in a country where rules about drinking alcohol, drugs and sex may be different from yours. Take extra precautions during your first few weeks at university.

NATIONAL HEALTH SERVICE (NHS)

The United Kingdom has a nationally funded health service – the National Heath Service (NHS). Most people use the free National Health Service which provides a wide range of medical treatment to all UK residents through a variety of means. Most of the services are free but for some there is a charge which you can claim back. The NHS website is: www.nhs.uk

Eligibility for NHS treatment

You will need to meet certain requirements to qualify for free NHS treatment. Students from EEA countries and from those countries that have a reciprocal health agreement with the UK (see below) are entitled to receive free healthcare regardless of the duration of their stay here in the UK. All international students and their dependants studying on a course of more than six months (any duration in Scotland) are also entitled to free healthcare. If your course lasts for less than six months (or you are not from an EEA nation) and your country does not participate in a reciprocal healthcare agreement then you will not be entitled to receive free treatment except in emergencies. You should have adequate insurance for the total duration of your stay here as a student, because private health treatment can be very expensive. It is better to take out health or travel insurance in your home country that covers your medical expenses in the UK, as very few companies offer medical insurance to students staying in the UK for less than a year. EEA nationals and their dependants staying in the UK for less than six months should fill out the form E128 in their country of residence. This will enable them to receive full NHS treatment.

RECIPROCAL HEALTHCARE AGREEMENT

Britain has reciprocal health agreements with the following countries: All EEA countries, Anguilla, Australia, Barbados, British Virgin Islands, Bulgaria, Channel Islands, Czech Republic, Falkland Islands, Gibraltar, Hungary, Isle of Man, Malta, Montserrat, New Zealand, Poland, Romania, Russia, St. Helena, Turks and Caicos Islands, former Soviet Union States, and all countries of the former Yugoslavia. Nationals of these countries are entitled to receive free healthcare under the NHS for the duration of their stay here.

All overseas students are entitled to receive NHS treatment if their course of study is for more than six months in England and Wales, or a course of any duration in Scotland. As you enter the country the immigration officer will ask you to register with the health authorities at the port of entry. You can register as a patient with your institution's health centre or your local surgery later.

REGISTERING WITH A DOCTOR

You should register with a doctor (also known as a general

practitioner or GP), as soon as possible when you arrive in the UK. Most universities and colleges will have their own health centres and you may be able to register there. Some universities and colleges charge a small fee for the service. If your institution does not have a health centre, register with a local doctor's surgery near to where you live.

To register, you will need to go to the surgery personally during consulting hours (9.00am to 5.00pm) and register as an NHS patient. Most surgeries have both male and female doctors and should you prefer to be seen by a female doctor you can request one. You might be asked to show proof of your student status and your passport when you register. When accepted you will be sent a medical card showing your NHS number. You can contact your local health authority should you need any help in registering. Their address and telephone number can be obtained through your local post office or doctor.

Under the NHS, consultations with doctors are free both at the surgery or at home and (in the case of emergencies). If a doctor gives you a prescription for medication you will have to take it to your local pharmacist. Some medicines are available only on prescription and you might have to pay initially. To reclaim the money you will have to fill in form HC1 (obtainable at the doctor's surgery, pharmacists, the post office or your Student Advice Centre), enclose the receipts and claim the cost back from the NHS. Your International Office or Student Advice Centre will be able to advise you on how to fill in the form.

NHS DIRECT OR NHS 24
NHS Direct is a round-the-clock nurse advice and health

information service, providing confidential information on a wide
range of issues. The nurses are able to advise on health
conditions, local healthcare services and late night pharmacies.
There is also a confidential translation service if you wish to
describe your ailments in another language. You can call NHS
Direct in England and Wales on 0845 4647 or NHS 24 in
Scotland on 0800 224 488. NHS Direct and NHS 24 also operate
an online interactive enquiry service at www.nhsdirect.nhs.uk

DENTISTS AND OPTICIANS

Dentists

Dental treatments are very expensive in the UK. You will need to
register with a dentist under the NHS to qualify for NHS dental
treatment. A list of dentists providing NHS treatment is usually
available from your Student Advice Centre or your local post
office. Call or check first whether the dentist accepts NHS patients
as some dentists will only accept private patients. You will then
have to give the dentist your NHS number (available on your
medical card). There is usually a charge for dental treatment.
Check in advance what the costs are going to be as costs for some
treatment (even under the NHS) can be very expensive. You may
be able to claim these charges back from the NHS by filling in
form HC1.

Opticians

In the UK general eyecare is provided by opticians who operate
from high street shops. You will have to pay for an eye test. If
you need glasses then the optician will give you a prescription.
The cost of glasses and contact lenses can be high and may vary
considerably from shop to shop and from brand to brand. If you

wear contact lenses or glasses then it might be better to get an additional pair from your home country before you leave. Popular high street opticians are Boots, Optical Express, Specsavers and Dolland and Aitchinson. Besides these there are also several local opticians listed in *Yellow Pages*.

PHARMACIES

Boots, Lloyds and Superdrug are the most popular high street pharmacists. They are usually open from 09.00am to 6.00pm Monday to Saturday and from 11.00am to 5.00pm on Sundays. Most of the supermarkets also have in-store pharmacies. In addition to the high street pharmacists there are several local pharmacies. Major towns and cities have 24-hour pharmacies and these are listed in the local *Yellow Pages*. You can also call NHS Direct on 08457 4647 or if you live in Scotland, NHS 24 on 0800 224 488. Pharmacists also provide advice on the treatment of minor health problems. This could save you a trip to your GP. All GP prescriptions are charged a flat fee of £6.50 per item by the pharmacist.

Free contraception

All prescribed contraceptives are free in the UK. Most Students' Unions supply free contraception through their student welfare department, Student Advice Centre and Nightline. You will also be able to get free condoms and contraception though local Health Promotion Units and some surgeries. Your Student Advice Centre or your local post office should have a list of them or you can find them online at www.fpa.org.uk

PRIVATE HEALTHCARE

Private healthcare is widely available in the UK but is generally very expensive. Expect to pay around £2,500 for a minor treatment. However, with private healthcare you get treated quickly and have certain facilities and comforts that are not available on the NHS, such as the privacy of your own en-suite room with TV.

Health insurance

The number of insurance companies offering health insurance has risen slowly in recent years. Private health insurance offers assurance of treatment available promptly in a private hospital. As a private patient you can often choose when and where treatment will take place. However, some illnesses (HIV, self-injury, alcohol and drug abuse) and treatments will not be covered by a private medical insurance policy and these are explained in the policy documents. You still need to be registered with the NHS.

◆ AXA (www.axa.com or 0800 728 436)
◆ Norwich Union (www.norwichunion.com or 0800 056 2593)
◆ BUPA (www.bupa.com or 0800 600 500)

offer healthcare insurance to students staying for six months or longer in the UK.

Only Endsleigh Insurance (www.endsleigh.com or 0800 028 3571) offers medical insurance for treatment under the NHS to international students staying for less than six months with premiums starting from £20 per month.

Premiums vary according to your lifestyle, habits, age and the total length of your stay in the UK. By law, all insurers have to offer a cooling-off period (usually 14 days) from the date you take out the policy in case you change your mind. You are entitled to a full refund if you decide not to go ahead with the policy.

The Hospital Savings Association (www.hsa.co.uk or 01264 353 211), a non-profit organisation, helps its members to meet day-to-day expenses of hospitalisation even under the NHS. For a monthly premium, starting from £4, members get their costs met in the case of hospitalisation. You'll need to contribute monthly by direct debit for six months before you can claim any expenses towards your hospitalisation.

COUNSELLING SERVICES
Most universities and colleges have a free in-house counselling service where they offer short-term counselling on social skills, academic problems, loneliness, homesickness, confidence, cultural transition, anxiety, stress, phobias, and problems linked to drugs or alcohol. Private counsellors are expensive in the UK and usually charge from around £50 for an hourly session.

VACCINATIONS
You do not need any vaccinations to enter the UK. Currently all students under 25 receive the meningitis C vaccination before the beginning of the academic term. You should try to get a tetanus and meningitis C injection before you leave for the UK. You can also get this vaccination free of charge at your university health centre or surgery at the beginning of term.

BRINGING HEALTH RECORDS TO THE UK

In accordance with immigration requirements you may be asked to undergo a health check with a local British Embassy or High Commission accredited doctor in your home country when you apply for a student visa. You'll also be asked to have a chest X-ray taken which you will need to carry with you when you come to the UK. You will be asked to go through the port health control unit where you will have to show it to the port health officer. You may encounter a few delays if you do not have your X-ray with you. You will also be asked to fill in a form on which you will be required to write your UK address. You can post the application later if you have not yet confirmed your accommodation in the UK.

You should also bring your medical and prescription records with you. If you are taking regular medication in your home country it might be sensible to bring a supply of the medication when you come to the UK. Do check whether it is licensed to be used in the UK (www.hmcr.gov.uk) and bring it in a correctly labelled (in English) container.

HEALTH ISSUES IN THE UK

Although you are unlikely to catch anything more serious than a cold or the flu, the following are some of the health issues that you need to be aware of.

Meningitis

Meningitis is a rare brain infection that mainly affects people under 25 years of age. The time you are at the highest risk of catching meningitis is during the first few weeks at university. Students under 25 and those living in a hall of residence should take extra precautions against meningitis C during the first few weeks at the university.

Hepatitis

Hepatitis A: Hepatitis A is an infection of the liver caused by the Hepatitis A virus. It is mainly spread because of poor personal hygiene. The disease is quite common in the UK and vaccinations are available at all surgeries.

Hepatitis B and C: Again, these are infections of the liver which are transmitted through bodily fluids. They could be caused through unprotected sex or using contaminated needles or blades. Currently, there is no vaccination available to protect against Hepatitis C.

Flu (influenza)

Flu is a viral infection of the lungs and the air passages and is quite common during winter, especially among students during the beginning of term. Symptoms include headaches, fever and other cold-like symptoms.

Hay fever

Hay fever is an allergic reaction to grass pollens in the air. Pollens are usually released by plants between May and September but are at their peak in June and July.

Chlamydia

Chlamydia is one of the most common sexually transmitted infections in the UK. Caused by the bacteria chlamydia trachomatis, it spreads among people who have unprotected sex.

USEFUL TELEPHONE NUMBERS

NHS Direct:	0854 4647 (24 hours)
NHS 24 (Scotland):	0800 224 488 (24 hours)
Health Information Service:	0800 665 544 (24 hours)
Alcoholics Anonymous:	0845 769 7555
Pregnancy Advice Service:	0845 730 4030
Drinkline:	0800 917 8282
	(9.00am to 11.00pm, Monday to Friday)
National Drugs Helpline:	0800 7766 600 (24 hours)
Stop Smoking:	0800 917 8896 (24 hours)
Samaritans:	08457 90 90 90 (24 hours)
Sexwise:	0800 282 930
Family Planning:	0845 310 1334
	(9.00am to 6.00pm, Monday to Friday)

IMPORTANT WEBSITES

www.nhs.uk

The website for the National Health Service has detailed information on treatments, a self-help guide, a health encyclopaedia as well as topical features and news on health issues in the UK. The website also offers a comprehensive directory search of all doctors, dentists, pharmacies and opticians in the UK.

www.patient.co.uk

Another good website on health matters with information, advice and links to other sites. The site also contains more than 600 leaflets on health that GPs in the UK give to their patients during consultations.

www.studenthealth.co.uk

Offers information and downloadable advice leaflets on student health issues in the UK. The website also has a directory of University Health Centres in the UK.

www.fpa.org.uk
A sexual health website that offers information and advice on sexual health. The website also has a list of local units where you can get free contraception.

www.ndh.org.uk
The National Drug Help website (also known as talktofrank) offers confidential online advice on issues related to drugs. The website also has a post code search facility for local organisations where counselling and support for drug addiction are available.

www.mind.org.uk
A mental health website giving information and support for mental health related problems. The website also has downloadable leaflets and books on coping with mental distress.

www.samaritans.org.uk
The website of the Samaritans – an organisation that provides free and confidential emotional support for people who are experiencing feelings of self-harm or suicide. They also operate by email (jo@samaritans.org.uk) and usually get back to you within 24 hours.

6

Employment

Most students work while studying in the UK. The cost of living in Britain is generally high so a steady source of income can help you with your expenses. The experience of working in a different culture and environment can also be very rewarding. Traditionally, students do unskilled jobs such as working in bars, shops, fast food outlets, restaurants and supermarkets.

EEA NATIONALS
All EEA nationals and their dependants can work freely without any restrictions during their stay in the UK. However, nationals of the eastern and central European accession countries (Czech Republic, Estonia, Hungary, Latvia, Lithuania, Poland, Slovakia, and Slovenia) need to register with the Home Office (under the Worker Registration Scheme) as soon as employment begins.

NON-EEA NATIONALS AND WORK PERMITS

International students can now work without a work permit while studying, as long as they are not prohibited from doing so on their entry clearance or visa. However, there are still some restrictions on the type and hours of work that they can do. They are not allowed to work for more than 20 hours per week during term time, except where a work placement is to be undertaken as a necessary part of the course of study as agreed by the institution. They cannot engage in business, self-employment, the provision of services or take up work as a professional entertainer or sportsperson. They should not pursue a career by filling a permanent full-time vacancy. During vacations they are permitted to work full-time (40 hours).

Occasionally a student may have a prohibition on working stamped in their passport. This will indicate that they have 'Leave to enter for/until (a specified time). No work or recourse to public funds.' Check your visa before seeking work.

Dependants

The immigration rules allow the spouse or dependent child of a non-EEA international student to work without a work permit. Note, however, that the spouse or child of a student will be prohibited from working unless leave to enter has been given for 12 months or more.

Work experience and internships

As part of your course you are allowed to take a sandwich placement provided you are at a recognised university or college; the placement is essential if you are to obtain your qualification; the placement is a small part of your total course duration; and will not go on beyond the course completion date.

WHERE TO FIND WORK

The best place to look for part-time work is at your institution's careers advisory service, local job centre, local employment agencies, local press, local shop windows and employer stalls at your university freshers fair.

The careers advisory service usually has a list of all part-time jobs available in and around the university or college campus. Check your Students' Union as they tend to employ a lot of casual student staff to work in the bars, shops and catering. Working on the campus or in the Students' Union might also help you to save time because you do not have to commute to work in the town or city.

Your local job centre, run by the government, will have listings of available jobs in your town. They will even interview you on the spot and confirm your appointment.

Local employment agencies advertise both full-time and part-time jobs. Call them or drop in to arrange an appointment. Take your passport, CV and references if you have any. You will then be interviewed by one of the representatives. It is best to visit as many agencies as possible to increase your chances of finding employment. Major national recruitment agencies are Manpower, Hays Personnel, Reed and Kelly's Services. Besides these there are several local recruitment agencies listed in *Yellow Pages*.

It is also worth walking around your town or city to check notices in the windows of supermarkets, shops and restaurants, or enquire inside. Most of these establishments tend to employ part-time and casual staff especially before Christmas. Start looking for jobs during late September and October.

Prospective employers will ask to see your ID, passport and visa to check whether you are permitted to work in the UK.

Before accepting a job, make sure that you are aware of the commitments being asked of you. Remember that you are in the UK to get your academic qualifications and if you commit to too much work you may find your studies being affected. Also be sure that you are aware of when and how much you are being paid. You should receive a contract outlining pay, hours of work and further details about the employer.

When you start work your employer will take a photocopy of your ID/passport and visa. You'll also be asked to provide your National Insurance number and to fill in certain tax forms (see below).

WAGES

Do not expect to be paid much for casual or part-time work. The current national minimum wage is £4.85 per hour (if you are aged 22 or over) and £4.10 per hour (if you are under 22). Most organisations pay around £5.50 an hour. However, some establishments pay extra for work done during unsociable hours (after 8.00pm) and pay double for work on Sundays and bank holidays.

NATIONAL INSURANCE AND TAX

National Insurance numbers

Everyone who works in the UK requires a National Insurance (NI) number. You do not need one before you start working so should ask your employer to issue you with a temporary NI number following the CA28 guide.

National Insurance numbers are issued by the Department of Work and Pensions (DWP). Getting an NI number can sometimes be frustrating. Call the National Insurance helpline on 0845 302 1479 and give them your UK residential address and employment details to find out where your local DWP Office or Job Centre Plus Office is. You can also locate one online at www.dwp.gov.uk or www.jobcentreplus.gov.uk or in the telephone directory (under government buildings).

You will need to apply for an NI number at the Social Security Office or Job Centre Plus Office. You will need to contact them first by telephone to make an appointment. You'll then be sent a letter confirming the appointment date and time along with the details of the documents required.

You will need to take your passport, proof of address (a letter or bill sent to your address in the UK), a letter from your employer confirming your employment and proof of your student status. The interview usually takes around an hour. You will then get a letter from a member of staff at the Social Security Office or Job Centre Plus confirming that you have applied for an NI number. You will then be sent your NI number by the Department and Work and Pensions. The number will be issued on a plastic card and will be made up of numbers and letters e.g. SX 12 34 56 C. It can take up to eight weeks for an NI number to be issued.

Tax and National Insurance payments

Generally speaking, the company you are working for will deal with all your tax and National Insurance payments through the PAYE (pay as you earn) system. As a student you are liable to pay tax and National Insurance once you have passed the relevant thresholds, although most international students do not earn enough in a financial year to pay tax. You have to pay tax on any income over £91.25 per week or £4,745 in a tax year. The tax year in the UK begins on 6 April and runs up to 5 April of the following year. You'll have to pay National Insurance once your income is over £67 per week. Rates vary for those with dependants or a disability.

Annual income tax rates

◆ Personal tax-free allowance: £4,895.

◆ The lower rate (10%) is payable on the first £2,020 of income over the personal allowance.

◆ The basic rate (22%) is payable on income between £2,020 and £31,400 over the personal allowance.

◆ The higher rate (40%) is payable on income more than £31,400 over the personal allowance.

◆ All emergency tax is taxed at a basic rate allowance of 22%.

Tax and National Insurance payment calculations are very complicated and are based on your PAYE tax code. If you think you might be paying tax or NI unnecessarily, seek advice from the Citizens Advice Bureau, your college or university's advice centre or your local tax office.

If you are working for an employer during vacation time only, you can fill in a form P38 (S), which confirms your student status and stops tax deduction.

If you are working for two or more different employers, you will probably find that you are paying tax on both jobs. If your total income is still less than the tax thresholds, you can either reclaim this tax at the end of the tax year or arrange with the Inland Revenue to split your personal allowances between the jobs. Seek advice from the Citizens Advice Bureau, your college or university's Student Advice Centre or your local tax office.

EMPLOYMENT RIGHTS

If you work while studying it will probably be on either a part-time or casual basis. The difference between the two is that for the casual worker there is no mutuality of obligation. That is, you are free to work when you want to and the employer is free to offer work when she or he wants.

You are entitled to a written statement of particulars, which should detail:

- the names of the employer and employee;

- the date when the employment began and the period of continuous employment;

- the scale and rate of remuneration, how often the employee will be paid and the method of calculation;

- terms and conditions relating to hours of work and holiday entitlement (including public holidays);

- the job title or description; and

- the employee's place of work.

Casual workers, however, do not have a right to holiday pay, sick pay or other benefits. Part-time workers do have these rights, so wherever possible it may be better to obtain part-time status when applying for work.

Part-time workers also have the right to: access the company sick pay scheme; payment of severance pay; service supplements acquired after longer service. They also have the right to overtime rates of pay but only after they have completed the 'full-time' hours.

A part-time worker will have to give notice to leave, and this will either be agreed in your contract or will be the equivalent of one pay period (that is, if you are paid weekly you will give one week's notice). Although casual workers technically have to give notice, they do have the right to refuse any work offered.

You are always entitled to receive payment for work done. If, for any reason, deductions are made from your wages or pay is withheld, seek advice from the International Office, Citizens Advice Bureau or your student advice centre.

Forms

P38 (S)
P38 (S) is a form for full-time students working during vacations only. The student needs to fill in their course details, along with his or her address and NI number and hand it over to the employer. The form confirms the student status and prevents tax from being deducted.

P45

P45 is a record of your earnings, tax deduction and NI contributions from your previous job. Your P45 will confirm the total amount of pay you have received in the current tax year, the total tax paid, your income tax code and your total National Insurance contributions.

When you leave a job you are given a P45 by your employer. Keep this safe and give this form to your new employer when you start a new job. Your new employer will then send part of it off to their tax office and will help them in calculating your tax contributions.

P46

P46 is a form which your employers will ask you to fill in if you do not have a P45. The tax office will allocate you a tax code and your employer will then deduct tax according to the tax code.

P60

P60 is a detailed record of your earnings, tax deductions and NI contributions for the previous tax year. At the end of every tax year, your employer will give you a P60. Keep this safe as it is the only recordable document of your taxable income and NI contributions. It is difficult to obtain another copy.

Working illegally

The consequences of working in violation of your 'leave given', illegally or without a work permit (when one is required) can be severe. You risk receiving a fine, deportation or even imprisonment and this might affect your studies in the UK.

GLOSSARY OF TAX AND NI TERMS

National Insurance: A tax charged on income in the UK that is used to finance state benefits (health, pensions, etc.). Your National Insurance contribution is payable on top of income tax.

PAYE: Pay As You Earn. PAYE is a system which almost all employees use in the UK to pay their income tax. The employer deducts tax directly from wages or salary before they are received. An employer is responsible for sending tax to the tax office.

Personal Tax Allowance: This is the most that an individual can earn before paying income tax. For the current financial year this is £4,895.

Tax code: This is provided by the tax office and shows the allowances one can receive under the PAYE system. The tax code has three digits followed by a letter e.g. 494T.

USEFUL TELEPHONE NUMBERS

Revenue and Customs:	0845 915 7006
Work Permits UK:	0114 259 4074
DfES:	0870 000 2288.
Home Office:	0870 606 7766
Citizens' Advice Bureau:	020 7833 2181
	(The operator will then give your local CAB number)
Commission for Racial Equality:	0870 240 3697
Equal Opportunities Commission:	0845 601 5901
TUC (Know your rights line):	0870 600 4882
Lesbian and Gay Employment Rights:	020 7704 8066

USEFUL WEBSITES

www.ind.homeoffice.gov.uk

The website of the Home Office has complete information and guidance on immigration regulations and employment restrictions.

The site also has details about the Workers' Registration Scheme for nationals of eight Accession States of the EU.

www.workpermits.gov.uk
This government-run website has complete information and guidance about working in the UK.

www.unison.org.uk
Unison is the largest trade union in Britain and represents people who work in public services, voluntary and private sectors. The website has many publications, articles and documents on employees' rights while at work.

www.tuc.org.uk
The website of the Trade Union Congress (TUC). The TUC represents workers from 70 affiliated unions and campaigns for a fair deal at work. The website has useful downloadable leaflets on your rights at work.

www.adviceguide.org.uk
The website of the Citizens Advice Bureau. This has much useful information about rights at work, pay and other statutory rights. The website also has local addresses and telephone numbers where free and confidential information and advice can be obtained on employment matters.

www.hmrc.gov.uk
The website of Customs and Excise where all the information on tax and NI contributions can be found. This website has a special section for students and their tax matters.

www.cre.gov.uk
The Commission for Racial Equality is a government body that works to prevent racial discrimination, harassment and abuse. The website has downloadable publications on equal rights for all at work. It also operates a confidential advice service.

www.eoc.org.uk
The Equal Opportunities Commission is an organisation working to stop sex discrimination at work in the UK. The website describes in detail rights for men and women at work.

www.disability.gov.uk
The Disability Rights Commission website advises on the rights of disabled people and the legislation for disabled people and their rights that exist in the UK.

$$\boxed{7}$$

Money

"I'm doing a degree in
understanding student finance."

Careful financial planning is necessary for a productive student life in the UK. Students – a group with high expenses and limited income – are famously needy. To paraphrase Errol Flynn, students' problems lie in reconciling their gross habits with their net income. Money and finance in Britain could be quite different from other countries and a good working knowledge of them should make your student life hassle-free. Remember, this is probably the first time that you have lived away from your family and the first time you have had to manage a budget of your own.

Although students aren't expected to make much money, financial woes could impede your academic performance. It could also land you with large and unnecessary debts, which could affect your later working life.

Money is an important business for all students, but foreign students can have an additional problem: dealing with two currencies, expenses in pounds but receipts in another currency. You could plan your expenses properly, but through no fault of your own have budget upsets due to foreign exchange rate swings.

BRINGING MONEY FROM HOME

Do not bring large sums in cash as this can be dangerous. A small amount in pounds to cover your initial expenses for at least a week should be sufficient. It is advisable to bring large sums of money in the form of a sterling banker's draft, Sterling travellers' cheques, or you could transfer money after you have opened a bank account in the UK.

BANK ACCOUNTS

It is very useful to have a bank account whilst studying in the UK and it is important to choose one carefully. It is cheaper to have a UK bank account to manage your expenses in the UK, to have your wages paid into if you want to work and for immigration purposes if you need to extend your visa in the UK. Also, before you depart for the UK, check with your local bank whether they have any agreement with banks in the UK, how easy it will be to transfer money from your country and whether or not there are any charges.

Choosing the right bank

The four major banks that control nearly two thirds of current accounts in the UK are HSBC, Royal Bank of Scotland/NatWest group, Barclays and Lloyds TSB. Other banks are HBOS (Halifax Bank of Scotland), Co-operative Bank, Abbey and the Alliance & Leicester. Besides these, there are regional banks in Northern

England, Northern Ireland and Scotland. They are: Yorkshire
Bank, Northern Bank, Ulster Bank, Bank of Ireland and
Clydesdale Bank.

Most universities will have at least one or a limited number of
banks on campus. Do not go to the first bank you come across.
Shop around. Check the bank stalls during the freshers fair. Look
into their interest rates, charges, and the facilities that they offer.
Check how far the branch is from your campus or home. Ask
other students who have bank accounts before you make your
choice.

Types of account

Banks in the UK offer various types of account. The main two
types are current accounts and savings accounts. Current accounts
are ideal as they have no restrictions on deposit or withdrawal of
funds. A savings account may have some restriction on the
withdrawal of funds but will offer a higher rate of interest. If you
have a large amount of money then it is worth putting most of it
into a high-interest savings account and transfering it to your
current account according to your requirements.

Interest and facilities

All banks offer a free current account facility which means you
should not pay anything provided you are in credit. Most banks
offer minimal interest on money in the student account. At
present, interest rates offered vary from 0.10 per cent to 0.25 per
cent. However, Halifax Bank of Scotland (HBOS) and Alliance &
Leicester offer around 3% interest if the minimum deposit or
balance per month is over £1,000.

Most banks have now stopped offering incentives to foreign students to open a student account with them as they see foreign students as non-profitable. Currently, HSBC offers the best deal to overseas students. Students get a Young Persons Railcard valid for four years (worth about £80) or £50 in cash when opening an account, the facilities of a Switch/Maestro card (debit card), cheque guarantee card, a chequebook, credit card and interest-free overdraft (depending on how your account is run). NatWest and the Royal Bank of Scotland offer a Solo card (debit card), chequebook, and credit card after six months but no overdraft facilities to international students. Barclays and Lloyds offer a current account Visa Electron card (debit card), but no chequebook or overdraft facility. Both Barclays and Lloyds TSB permit overseas students to apply for a credit card after two years of running a current account. Some banks' facilities, including Barclays, Lloyds TSB, the Co-operative Bank and Alliance & Leicester, can also be accessed through post offices located throughout the country.

All banks now offer free telephone and internet banking which is worth having to check real time balances, to transfer money and for the day-to-day management of your finances.

BUILDING SOCIETIES

Unique to Britain, Building Societies are owned by the customers (members). They do not offer any student accounts but students are allowed to open a normal account with them. They offer a slightly higher rate of interest than the banks and are non-profit making. Popular building societies in the UK are Nationwide, Leeds and Yorkshire.

Banking systems and charges

Banks and building societies in the UK are generally open from 9.30am to 5.00pm, Monday to Friday, and some open from 9.30am to 12 noon on Saturday. These are the standard opening times. Some banks are open all day on Saturday as well. High street branches will operate full banking facilities while branches on campus might offer limited facilities. Cheques usually take around three to five days to clear. The quickest and most convenient way to pay your bills is by direct debit.

Not all banking facilities in the UK are free. Setting up direct debits, standing orders and paying in cash or by cheques are all free. Withdrawing money from your UK bank account from most cash machines is also free. However, do bear in mind that there are fee-charging cash machines located in some shopping centres, post offices and night clubs. These charge around £1.50 per withdrawal. You will be advised on screen before the withdrawal about the charges and you can cancel the transaction. You can also withdraw money through the cash back facility offered by most retailers when you pay for goods or services by UK debit card. The minimum cash back is £10 and the maximum allowed is £50.

Other charges vary from bank to bank and it is worth checking with them before you use the facilities. There will most likely be charges for the misuse of bank accounts, such as going overdrawn without funds in your account. Missing a direct debit and standing order can also bring a high charge – around £30, plus interest. If you are charged for misuse then talk to the bank and explain to them the reasons. They may waive the charges. Banks also charge for other services they offer. These include sending money abroad, purchasing a bankers' draft and the processing of foreign cheques.

Chip and PIN

Almost all retailers now accept Chip and PIN cards in the UK. When paying for purchases your card will be inserted into a verifying machine. Instead of signing you will be asked to enter your PIN number using the key pad. If your card does not have the Chip and PIN facility then you will have to sign the receipt and hand it back to the retailer.

Opening a student account

Opening a bank account is very straightforward. Contact your local branch and ask for an appointment with a customer services adviser. In some branches you may be able to see them straight away. You will need to take the following with you to the branch:

◆ Your passport or your National Identity Card (If you are an EEA national).

◆ A letter confirming your student registration from your college or university. This needs to be addressed to the bank manager of the bank you wish to open an account with.

◆ Your proof of address. This could be a letter from your hall office, a letter from your university, a tenancy agreement if you live in rented accommodation or a utility bill with your name and address on it. Some banks will also ask for proof of your address in your home country and statements from your bank account.

A customer services adviser will ask you a few details before the account opening process is completed. You'll receive your cash or debit card, PIN number, cheque book and account details by post around five days later. You might encounter some difficulties or a slight delay in opening a bank account if you are in the UK for less than six months or are under a list of nationalities that require further money laundering checks.

List of banks and their contact details

Abbey	Tel: 0845 765 4321
	www.abbey.com
Alliance & Leicester	Tel: 0500 95 95 95
	www.alliance-leicester.co.uk
Bank of Ireland	Tel: 08457 365 333
	www.bank-of-ireland.co.uk
Bank of Scotland	Tel: 08457 801 801
	www.bankofscotland.co.uk
Barclays	Tel: 0800 99 44 22
	www.barclays.co.uk
Clydesdale	Tel: 08457 24 00 24
	www.clydesdalebank.co.uk
Co-operative Bank	Tel: 0845 600 6000
	www.co-operativebank.co.uk
Halifax	Tel: 08457 203 040
	www.halifaxonline.co.uk
HSBC	Tel: 0800 130 130
	www.hsbc.co.uk
LloydsTSB	Tel: 0800 096 9799
	www.lloydstsb.com
National Westminster Bank	Tel: 08456 013 366
	www.natwest.com
Royal Bank of Scotland	Tel: 08457 222 345
	www.rbs.co.uk
Woolwich	Tel: 0800 33 44 99
	www.woolwich.co.uk
Yorkshire Bank	Tel: 08457 365 365
	www.yorkshirebank.co.uk

GLOSSARY OF BANKING TERMS

Automated credit transfer: A method of direct payment to your bank account instead of paying by cheque or cash.

Automated teller machines (ATM): Also known as cash machines, these allow you to withdraw money and perform other account functions using your debit, credit or cash card.

Balance: The amount in your account at any given time. This can be in credit or overdrawn.

Cash card: A card issued by your bank to allow you to withdraw money from your account. However, you cannot use it as debit card or to guarantee cheques.

Charge card: Similar to a credit card but the account holder receives a statement at the end of month which he or she has to settle in full.

Cheque guarantee card: A facility available on some debit cards. Cheques are guaranteed by the bank up to the monetary limit displayed on the card.

Cirrus: Cirrus is an international network of cash machines that allows you to withdraw money in different countries.

Credit card (Amex, JCB, Diners, MasterCard or Visa): A card through which you pay for goods and services by credit.

Current account: Similar to a checking account. A bank account that is normally used for daily transactions (for example, making payments either by a debit card or cheque, direct debits and standing orders). This type of account pays little interest but has no restrictions on withdrawal or deposits.

Debit card (Switch/Maestro, Solo, Visa Delta and Visa Electron): A card through which you can pay for goods and services. The money spent is automatically withdrawn from your account.

Direct debit: A payment from a bank account arranged by the receiver with permission from the account holder.

Interest: The charge made to you if you borrow money or the income you receive if you invest it in a bank account.

LINK: LINK is a British network of cash machines that allows you to withdraw money in the UK only.

Maestro: An international payment system that allows you to pay for goods and services using your debit card.

Overdraft: A facility through the current account that permits you to borrow up to an agreed amount for an agreed amount of time.

PIN: A personal identification number issued by the bank for use with a cash card, credit card or debit card.

Savings account: An account with a bank or financial institution which pays higher interest rates on balances held. The amount of interest depends on the amount of money in the account and the notice period required for withdrawals. In most cases the longer the notice period, the higher the interest rate.

Store card: Store cards are very similar to credit cards but are issued by retail stores. Their use is restricted to the stores that issue them. They charge a higher rate of interest, usually around 25 per cent.

Standing Orders: An instruction by a bank's customer to the bank to pay a regular amount of money into another account.

Visa Plus: An international network of cash machines, managed by VISA, that allows you to withdraw money anywhere in the world.

BUDGETING

As an overseas student with limited access to local funding you will need to budget to ensure that you have enough funds throughout your stay in the UK. This is probably the best way of calculating your financial needs and gives you a complete picture of your financial affairs. Most colleges and universities, the NUS and various banks offer an online budget planner which should help you to list and understand your income and expenditure. Budget planners should also be available in paper format from your Student Advice Centre.

You will also have to take into account that your income and expenditure may differ from term time to vacation time. While planning to budget bear in mind that some months can be more expensive than the others e.g. winter, or during vacations when you want to go back home. Your biggest expense will be your fees, followed by rent, food, as well as study and leisure expenses. While budgeting remember to be realistic and not to overestimate your income. Try to look for ways to avoid spending too much money. The tips on saving below and the budget planner at the end of this chapter should help you.

TIPS ON SAVING

1. **Buy in charity shops or second-hand.**
   There are plenty of charity shops in every town and city around the UK. Charity shops sell second-hand books, clothes, CDs, furniture and other items donated by the public.

2. **Shop around for special offers and promotions.**
   Most supermarkets have special offers (like BOGOF: Buy One Get One Free, multisave packs, coupon promotions etc.) going on throughout the year. Try to minimise your expenses by buying promotional items and sharing them with your friends.

3. **Bring a packed lunch to university or college**
   Although shops and restaurants on campus are comparatively cheap, you can still save money by bringing a packed lunch to campus. Campus catering facilities permit students to eat packed lunches on the premises. Most of them even offer cutlery and the use of a microwave to warm your food.

4. **Keep a record of daily spending**
   This will help you to get a glimpse of your spending habits and to minimise expenses.

5. **Get a part-time job**
   Most students work while studying in the UK. A part-time job will help with your expenses whilst in the UK.

6. **Make the most of your NUS student card for discounts**
   According to research carried out by NUS, students save more than £500 by

regularly using their NUS student card. Almost all the high street shops, restaurants, bars, cinemas, nightclubs etc. offer a 10–20 per cent student discount. You'll need to produce your NUS student card at the till in order to claim the discount – so remember to carry it in your wallet at all times.

7. Other tips

Avoid taking taxis, or if you have to, share one with your friends. Buying all the books on your course booklist will be expensive. Find out which ones are essential by asking your tutor and other students. Use the library rather than buying books, or if you have to buy books try second-hand shops or buy books from the seniors in your department.

FINANCIAL DIFFICULTIES

If you encounter any unforeseen financial difficulties then contact your International Office, Student Advice Centre or the Citizens Advice Bureau immediately. Most colleges and universities administer a hardship fund or loan for international students. Universities also have a list of local charities that might be able to help you. UKCOSA (www.ukcosa.org.uk) has produced a guide on sources of funding for international students. EEA students, depending upon their situation, might be able to claim some funds from the government.

WHAT WOULD IT COST YOU?

The following are prices of items you may need during your stay here in the UK. These prices are intended as a guide only. Prices vary regionally in the UK and are around 10–15 per cent cheaper in Scotland, Northern Ireland and Northern England. Prices vary locally as well. Remember it is cheaper to buy from supermarkets or local markets than from corner shops.

- Meals: a normal lunch costs about £3.
- Take-away meals (Indian, Chinese and other): £6.
- Beer: £5 for eight cans (500 ml each in supermarkets), £2.75 for a pint in a pub, £2.50 for a 300 ml bottle in a club. Some clubs have cheaper student nights.
- Chocolate bar: from 40p.
- Fast food meal (burgers): £3.50.
- Pizza: from £6.99 for 9″ pizza.
- Can of soft drink: 50p.
- Bottled water: 60p.
- Coffee/tea/chocolate (a regular cup): £1.50.
- Ready meals: £3.50.
- Bus ticket: £1.20 upwards depending upon the distance.
- Cigarettes: from £3.80 to £5.10 for a packet of 20.
- Condoms: £2 for a pack of three.
- Hair cut: from £10 for men and up to £40 for women.
- Shampoo: £2.50.
- Toothbrush: £1.50.
- Toothpaste (100g): £2.
- Photographic film: £3.50 for 24 pictures.
- Developing costs for photos: from £3.99.
- Milk: 40p for one pint.
- Bread: 50p for a loaf.
- Chips (small portion): £1.
- CD: £7–£15.
- DVD: £10–£17.
- Newspapers: 60p on weekdays and £1.20 on Saturdays and Sundays at newsagents (and 20p on weekdays at the Students' Union shop).
- Cinema: £6.50 without student ID, £4.50 with student ID.
- Movie rental: £4 per night for new releases and £2.75 for others.
- Petrol: 95p a litre.
- Diesel: 98p a litre.

Budget planner

The planner below should help calculate your income and expenditure.

INCOME	£	EXPENDITURE	£
		Rent	
Parental/family support		Gas (if any)	
Earnings		Electricity (if any)	
Grant/bursary		Water (if any)	
Benefits		Council tax (if liable)	
Sponsorship		Travel (within your city)	
Trusts/charities		Travel (home)	
Other income		Insurance	
		Rentals	
		TV licence	
TOTAL		Telephone (including mobile)	
DEBTS (if any)	**£**	Food (and housekeeping)	
List creditors and total amount outstanding here	List current repayments here	Laundry	
		Course costs (books and equipment)	
		Clothes	
		Medical costs	
		Socialising	
		Dependants' costs (if applicable)	
		Other expenses	
TOTAL		**TOTAL**	

8

University Life

SETTLING IN TO UNIVERSITY LIFE

The great thing about studying in the UK is not just the academic curriculum, but also the splendid chance for all the extra-curricular activities that are available to students. Participating in these will make you a well-rounded personality and could render you more attractive to a prospective employer. If you make full use of the sports, entertainment and music facilities, you are less likely to miss home. You can also make great friends, and will appreciate life in the UK much more. You can learn about other cultures and people, and maybe even learn a new language or two.

International week

Held at the beginning of the term, most universities and colleges organise an international week just before freshers week to welcome international students and to help them to get oriented with the campus, its facilities and the country. Lots of social events are organised during this week and you will also meet other international students as well as university staff.

During international week you will probably enrol on your course within your department, register with the library, register with the Students' Union, join any clubs and societies you wish, get settled down in your hall or house, familiarise yourself with the departments and staff, register with the doctor, register with the police (if necessary) and familiarise yourself with the campus and town or city. A welcome pack with a programme of the week's events and lots of information relevant to your course, university and the town or city will be usually be given to you at registration.

Colleges and universities also organise day trips for international students to nearby places of importance during the term. Trips are either free or heavily subsidised. You'll usually be informed about this during the beginning of the term.

Freshers' week

The first week of the term in October is known as freshers' week. The Students' Union organises a variety of events during this week. At the freshers' fair, you'll get a chance to meet representatives from national and local companies, banks, insurance companies, cinemas, restaurants, etc. Many of them hand out attractive freebies that will be useful during your stay here. During the fair you'll also get a chance to meet the representatives of clubs and societies that you can join. You'll also meet the Students' Union sabbatical officers.

RAG Week

RAG (Raise and Give) week is a fundraising campaign organised by students around the country, usually during March, for the benefit of charities. During this week a number of fundraising activities are organised across campus to raise money for various charities.

Summer Ball

The Summer Ball is one of the biggest student events on campus, usually held in June, just before the end of the summer term. Aside from a good line up of bands, DJs and shows, the ball will also have lots of other attractions such as a funfair, games, photo shoots, casinos, etc. Tickets can be expensive however, and cost around £40.

Christmas Ball

This is another formal event held at the Students' Union just before the end of the first term.

Sports Federation Ball

This formal dinner and ball is held during March for the members of all clubs and societies. Individual and group achievements are recognised and awards are given for the best clubs and societies and their outstanding players.

Careers fair

Usually held during every term, the careers fair brings various companies to the campus. It gives you an ideal chance to speak to representatives of different companies and to find out more about working for them.

STUDENT SUPPORT ON CAMPUS

International Office

Apart from their usual enrolment duties, the International Office at most universities and colleges offer guidance and advice to international students on campus. The International Office is usually staffed by a team of international officers who are able to assist students on a wide range of matters.

Counselling service

Most colleges and universities will have a counselling service or at least a counsellor. Counsellors can provide help with any personal problems you might experience. Universities with a large proportion of international students will have an international and inter-cultural counsellor who is familiar with the emotional problems often experienced by international students.

Careers advisory service

Most universities and colleges have a careers advisory service to assist students in developing their careers. The centre advises students on finding part-time jobs for current students and offers a range of career-related services for graduates.

Student Advice Centre

There is usually an information and advice centre for students at the college and university. The advice centre operates a private and confidential service on a wide range of matters, including personal, immigration, financial and housing issues. The Student Advice Centre may be run by the Students' Union or by the university. Universities with a large proportion of international students will have an international student adviser.

Personal tutor or supervisor

At the beginning of term you will be assigned a personal tutor or supervisor who is there to listen to any problems of an academic nature that you may experience. They will also be able to tell you who can help you with any other problems.

Nightline

Nightline is a confidential telephone service run by students for students. The service usually operates between the hours of 7.00pm and 8.00am. You can call them if you are feeling alone or just need someone to speak to or would like some information. Their number is usually given to students during registration.

Study skills adviser

Universities and colleges have an adviser who can help with any problems you may have with writing essays or preparing for exams etc. They usually operate through the counselling service. General support for students in study methods, e.g. time management, note taking, preparing for presentations, revision and examination techniques is given by the study skills adviser.

English support programme/other foreign languages

The in-sessional programme supports those at the university or college whose first language is not English. Universities also offer short courses in foreign languages to students. Contact your department for further details.

STUDENT MEDIA

Student newspapers

Most of the universities and colleges have their own free student newspapers with complete editorial independence. Their main coverage is usually of student matters concerning the campus and town or city.

Student Times (weekly), *National Student* (monthly) and S*tudent Guardian* (weekly) are national student newspapers. *Student Guardian* is published every Thursday and covers a wide range of issues around the world, while *Student Times* and *National Student* concentrate on student life in Britain. They are available free from Students' Unions.

Student radio stations

Almost every campus has a student radio station transmitting mostly on an AM frequency, with a range of around three miles from campus. Many stations are also available via the internet. Student radio stations are student based and target a student audience. A full list of student radio stations in the UK can be obtained from www.studentradio.org.uk

Library

Universities and colleges in the UK have well stocked libraries on campus and most of them are open 24 hours a day during term time. Most libraries offer orientation tours and lectures to new students at the beginning of the term. Libraries on campus usually stock all the books on the reading list at a ratio of around one copy for every five students. You'll be issued with a library card at the beginning of term. The number of books you are permitted to borrow varies (usually around 30) according to your course. Libraries on campus also subscribe to a wide range of electronic periodicals that are available to the students.

As well as the above, libraries provide study rooms, computer rooms, book binding, video viewing, printing and photocopying services. A co-operative venture exists between all higher education libraries in the UK. You can borrow books or other materials from other academic libraries through inter-library loans. For further details contact your college or university library or check on to the web at www.uklibrariesplus.ac.uk

Computers and the internet

Your university or college usually provides you with free internet access on campus. You will be given a user name and password at the beginning of the term. Most universities and colleges have dedicated computer rooms with printers and scanners and most of them are open 24 hours. Many colleges and universities also offer wireless (WiFi) access on campus. Elsewhere, free internet access is also available at the council run libraries.

Catering on campus

Most campuses usually have several catering facilities where a wide variety of foods can be purchased at reasonable prices. Students are not charged value added tax (VAT) for food purchased on campus.

Most faculties on campus will have a common room both for staff and students where you can eat packed lunches. Campus catering facilities also permit students to eat packed lunches on the premises. Most of them even offer cutlery and the use of a microwave to warm your food.

The Students' Union

The Students' Union is usually located on campus. Within it, there are usually catering facilities, several bars serving alcohol and soft drinks, shops selling food, newspapers, magazines, cigarettes, stationery, cards, gifts and university-crested clothing. Unions might also run the Student Advice Centre, student newspaper and student radio station. Unions also manage all student groups and represent all students at the university, at both local and national levels. Full details of your Students' Union will be described in the Students' Union handbook, which you will be given at the freshers fair.

Sabbatical officers

The Students' Union is run by student sabbatical officers who are elected by the students. The governing body usually comprises a president, several vice presidents and executive officers.

International student representative

Most of the Students' Unions have an international student representative who co-ordinates the Students' Union's work with international students.

Entertainment in the Students' Union

The core of student entertainment is at your Students' Union. Throughout the year your Students' Union will host a wide variety of entertainment on its premises starting with freshers week. Bars and venues in the Students' Union are the hub of student social life. Regular events are held every weeknight including live bands, comedy performances, hip hop, cheese and jazz. Wednesday and Saturday nights at the union are popular with the home students. Unions also bring in high profile bands, DJs and other artists throughout the year. Not all events or evening entertainments in the Student's Union are free. Ticket prices for some of them vary from £3–£5.

International themed parties on campus
Throughout the year several international themed parties are held
by clubs affiliated to the Union. These include Greek parties,
Latin nights, Afro-Caribbean nights and Asian nights.

STUDY METHODS IN BRITISH COLLEGES AND UNIVERSITIES

The study system in the UK is likely to be different from the
system you are used to. Your course timetable will include a
mixture of lectures, seminars and tutorial groups. There will be
regular laboratory work for science students. A typical timetable
for a degree student will include approximately 12 to 20 hours per
week of actual teaching and an additional six hours of laboratory
work.

Educational culture in the UK is based on the principle that
students will develop independence and individuality. Great
emphasis is placed on the value of self-expression and originality.
You will be expected to participate actively in the learning
process. Students will be asked to present seminars, participate in
discussions and carry out group projects. It is accepted and
expected that students will openly disagree with academic staff
and provide their own ideas. Students are encouraged to develop
their critical and analytical skills. While lecturers will give you
reading lists, you are expected to read about topics yourself. You
will need to organise your own study time. You will be expected
to present material in a typed form. Remember, you are not
allowed to copy passages from books and other articles and put
them in your own work without attributing them to the original
author.

To support you in your studies you should be allocated a named academic tutor or supervisor who you will meet regularly during your academic year to discuss matters relating to your studies.

Assignments

During your course, you will be given assignments every term which will count towards your final grades. Your lecturers will notify you about the assignments and the deadlines. You should take deadlines for assignment work set by your tutors seriously. If you find that you are behind with a piece of work, then talk to your tutor about it. Don't ignore deadlines as that will affect your overall grading.

Exams

As a student you will have to take exams at the end of your academic year. The dates for the exams will vary according to your course. Exam details will be listed in the course handbook given to you at the beginning of the term. If you have a specific learning difficulty (e.g. dyslexia), disability or a medical problem then you may be granted certain allowances or extra time. Contact your institution's examinations office for further details.

Course representatives

Every course will have a course representative who represents students from your year. They play a very important role in letting the department know whether there are any problems or concerns about the course. If your course does not have a representative then contact the Students' Union or your Student Advice Centre directly.

GRADUATION

University graduation ceremonies usually take place twice a year, in July and January, with the majority of students graduating at the summer ceremony. Universities also permit students to graduate *in absentia*. In order to graduate you must have successfully completed your course and your name must appear on the official pass list. You should also have no outstanding debts owed to the university.

The university graduation office contacts all eligible students by the end of April. You'll need to confirm your attendance, reserve guest tickets and order your graduation gown and mortar board. Graduation is free but you'll have pay for hiring a gown and mortar board.

RELIGION

University campuses have facilities of worship for most religions. Most of them have an Anglican and Catholic chaplaincy and a prayer room for Muslims. Further details about places of worship are usually given during your welcome week or you can contact your International Office or Student Advice Centre. The Students' Union will also have several faith-based societies affiliated to it. Be aware that religious cults operate on campus and if you are approached by an individual or a group and are unsure what to do, seek advice from your International Office or Student Advice Centre.

EQUALITY

Universities have written policies on equality on campus. Everyone, whether staff or student, has a basic right to work and study without harassment, discrimination or insult. If you experience any form of discrimination then seek advice from your Student Advice Centre or your local Citizens Advice Bureau.

LGB GROUPS

An LGB society exists to provide political representation, support and campaign on behalf of lesbian, gay and bisexual students in the university. You can meet their representatives during the freshers' fair or at the Students' Union.

VOLUNTEERING

There are lots of opportunities for you to get involved in volunteering on campus or with local charities and organisations. They include working with other students, students with disabilities, working in charity shops, conservation projects, administration work, fundraising, counselling and coaching. Some universities also offer modular accreditation for any voluntary work done which is added to your transcripts.

SPORTS AND CLUBS

British universities and colleges place a great deal of importance on sport. Almost all the universities and colleges devote an entire Wednesday afternoon to sport and recreational activities. The most popular sport in UK universities and colleges is football. Rugby, hockey, athletics, cricket, canoeing and rowing are other popular sports. The clubs and societies office of your Students' Union organises several intramural and inter university sports programmes during the term in co-ordination with BUSA, the governing body of UK university sport.

You'll also find a wide range of non-sports (combined) clubs – and you'll probably find one that interests you (see below). From the agricultural club to the wine society, there is every opportunity to pursue an interest or hobby, or simply to try something new.

You can join clubs and societies during the freshers' fair or by visiting the club's office (usually located in the Students' Union). There will be a nominal membership fee. You can also form a sports club or a society of your own. Contact your Students' Union sports office for further information.

Sports clubs

Aikido, American football, athletics, basketball, boat club, break dance, canoe club, clay pigeon shooting, ladies' cricket, men's cricket, cycling, Christians in sport, dance, fencing, ladies' football, men's football, gliding, golf, hang gliding, ladies' hockey, men's hockey, kick boxing, kung fu, motor sports, mountaineering, netball, ninjutsu, polo, riding, rifle and pistol, lacrosse, ladies' rugby, men's rugby, sailing, ski club, squash, sub aqua, swimming, sky dive, table tennis, tae kwon do, tennis, volley ball, wing chum.

Combined clubs

African and Caribbean, agriculture, AISEC, Anime, Arab, archaeology, art, Asian, Botanika, Brazilian, Catholic, chess and bridge, Chinese, classics, conservation, Cypriot, drama, English, food, games, Hellenic, Indie, Japanese, Jewish, Labour, Latin American, law, music, Muslim, philosophy, politics, psychology, punk, rock, sci-fi, socialist, Singapore, Spanish, St John's Ambulance, theatre, wine, writers.

USEFUL WEBSITES

www.nus.org.uk or www.nusonline.co.uk

The National Union of Students (NUS) is a national organisation of students that represents the interests of all students in the UK. Almost all Students' Unions in the UK are affiliated to the NUS.

www.studentradio.org.uk

A representative and a support organisation for student radio stations in the UK. The website has links to all the student radio stations in the UK.

wwww.busa.org.uk

The British Universities Sports Association (BUSA) is the governing body of university sport in the UK. It is responsible for organising the inter-university sports programme. The website has complete details on each individual sport, its fixtures and results.

www.uklibrariesplus.ac.uk

UK Libraries Plus is a co-operative venture among the 125 higher education libraries. Members of this programme can use other academic libraries around the UK for the duration of the course.

$$\boxed{9}$$

Accommodation

A great place to stay will enrich your student life like nothing else. It can provide the environment you need for study as well as facilitate your relaxation. Many students make more friends in and around their place of residence than in the classrooms. A wise choice of accommodation can also save you time and money. Since many of you are away from your families, make sure you can create the best home away from home.

You should try to arrange your accommodation as soon as you are accepted on to a course. Most universities give priority to international students for places in halls of residence or other forms of student accommodation run by the University.

HALLS OF RESIDENCE

Living in halls or a private house has advantages and disadvantages. Most of the halls are on campus, fully furnished, run by the university for the students, with both fully-catered and self-catering facilities. If you live in a hall you do not need to worry about paying utility bills as the rent takes cares of it all. Your rooms and the common facilities (kitchens, bathrooms and toilets) are regularly cleaned and the security in the hall of residence is very good. Halls also offer rooms during term time only, thus saving you rent during vacations when you go back home. However, the rooms may be small, you might not like the food and it may not feel very homely being surrounded just by students.

Most of the rooms in halls of residence are single study bedrooms with shared common facilities. Universities do offer en-suite rooms but these will still have shared common facilities. Most universities have a policy where people of the same sex are placed in the same corridor where the facilities (kitchen, bathroom and toilets) are shared.

Universities have some halls of residence adapted to make them accessible for disabled students. All rooms offer a bed, wardrobe, bookshelves, desk and chair, desk lamp and bed linen. Rooms will also have a telephone and/or a high speed internet access for which there will be a reasonable charge.

Fully-catered
Almost all universities offer both self-catered and fully-catered facilities in their halls of residences. In a catered hall your rent includes the food. Catered halls serve food three times a day (breakfast, lunch and dinner) on weekdays and a limited service on weekends.

Catered halls have certain benefits. It saves you time and effort in cooking. The dining room is a place where a lot of students can socialise during meal times. However, the choice of food (vegetarian, ethnic and special meals) are very limited and they operate on restricted times. Breakfast is usually served between 7.30 and 8.30am, lunch between 12 noon and 2.00pm and dinner from 5.30pm to 7.00pm.

Self-catered

Halls of residence offering self-catering facilities have common kitchens – usually shared amongst eight people. The kitchens are fully equipped and provide fridges, freezers and cookers, as well as crockery, cutlery and cooking utensils. Self-catering accommodation might work out cheaper because you cook and eat your food when you want it and are not restricted to specified times.

Hall contents insurance

Most universities offer limited possessions insurance. The premium is included in the rent. Check with the hall office upon arrival. If you feel that the insurance cover is not enough then take out a private insurance. Premiums for contents insurance in halls start from £30 a year.

Facilities in the halls of residence

Most halls of residence have a common bar, TV room, computer room, a library or reading room and offer limited sports facilities. Halls also have coin-operated laundry facilities, a secure bike shed and storage facilities. Car parking is also available in most of the halls of residences but there may be a charge for it.

Warden or resident tutor

A warden or a resident tutor is available in each hall of residence for advice and help on your welfare. They should be your first point of contact with problems relating to your hall of residence.

Junior Common Room (JCR)

Most halls of residence have a Junior Common Room (JCR) where students can gather and socialise. The Junior Common Room usually has a bar, pool tables, games machines and a television.

Student committee

Every year students in hall elect a student committee, which is generally responsible for student welfare and entertainment in the hall. The committee organises social events such as Christmas and Summer Balls, films and trips. The committee also has an international representative.

Students with dependants

Most universities have facilities for accommodating international students with dependants. They usually offer individual flats on campus or shared houses with other student families. Contact your accommodation office before you arrive for information.

Rent in halls of residence

Rents in halls of residences vary around the UK with the South East and London region being the most expensive and Northern Ireland the cheapest. Rent for a standard room with shared facilities is the cheapest while an en-suite room costs around 30 per cent more. The following table is a guide only (for weekly rates).

Area	Fully-catered	Self-catered
South East	£90–£140	£60–£100
South West	£85–£130	£60–£90
Midlands	£80–£100	£55–£90
North England	£80–£100	£50–£85
Scotland	£80–£100	£50–£80
Northern Ireland	£65–£100	£45–£70

THE HOST SYSTEM

Host is a scheme that offers international students a chance to spend a few days in a British home, either near where they are studying or wherever they would like to visit in Britain. The visit will cost you nothing apart from your fares and you will get the opportunity to experience British home life. Details are available from your International Office, online at www.hostuk.org or directly from Host at 18 Northumberland Avenue, London, EC2N 5BJ. Tel: 020 7925 2595.

PRIVATE SHARED ACCOMMODATION

Private shared accommodation has certain benefits that a hall does not offer. If you decide to go for private accommodation you will need to find other students to share with you. The easiest way to find other students is by putting up notices around campus with your contact details. Accommodation offices have a 'find a flat-mate scheme', to help students who are looking for accommodation on their own. When you register with the scheme, the accommodation office puts you in touch with other students to form a group to search for appropriate private accommodation.

Rent

Rent varies from region to region with the South East and London areas being the most expensive. Rent varies according to the type of house and its proximity to campus. The following table is a guide only. Please note that rent does not include bills for services such as electricity, water, etc.

Area	Rent (per week)
South East	£50–£100
South West	£50–£85
Midlands	£45–£75
North England	£40–£65
Scotland	£40–£65
Northern Ireland	£40–£60

Finding a house

If you are looking for a house, then your first point of enquiry should ideally be at your university or college accommodation office where you will find a list of available properties. The office may also have further information about where to find houses. Look around the notice-boards in departments around the university and at the Students' Union as they occasionally have adverts for whole houses and spare rooms in shared houses.

Shops and newsagents located around your university campus usually advertise accommodation on cards in their windows. Properties to let are also advertised in the classifieds section of local newspapers.

Accommodation agencies around town can also be useful. There is normally a charge but only when you actually rent a property provided by them. Do not pay in any other circumstances. Properties let by agencies tend to be of better quality but you will be asked for references and undergo a further credit check. A full directory of letting agents is available on the web at www.ukpropertyshop.co.uk. They will also be listed in the local *Yellow Pages*.

House contents insurance
It advisable to take individual contents insurance when moving into private accommodation. Student houses are often targeted by thieves. Premiums for contents insurance start from around £30 a year.

House hunting
When you are house hunting with friends, make sure you all go to the house to look at it. What you think is acceptable may not be for others and *vice versa*. Do not go to view a property alone. It is advisable to read through housing packs provided by your Student Advice Centre. The booklet *Assured and assured shorthold tenancies: a guide for tenants* published by the Deputy Prime Minister's Office is a detailed guide for tenants and is available free from your Student Advice Centre or you can download it online at www.odpm.gov.uk

Try to speak to the previous tenants, if possible, away from the landlord. They will be the best source of information on potential problems in the house. Check the rooms have useable and useful furniture, such as desks, shelves etc. The kitchen should have a cooker, fridge, and decent ventilation. If there are more than six tenants there must be two bathrooms, with ventilators or windows in the house. Check for signs of damp or mould. Mould is often peeled off and painted over. Yellowing or bubbling paper or paint is a sign of an inherent mould problem. Check the landlord's gas safety record, and make sure it is current, as most houses in the UK have gas boilers for hot water and central heating. Find out when it was last serviced (they should be serviced annually by the gas board or a CORGI registered gas fitter). This must be updated every 12 months and the landlord is legally obliged to do this. It is a criminal offence if she or he does not.

Staining, discoloration or soot around the boiler or the gas fires is a sign of a leak or a fault and is very dangerous. The appliance could be leaking carbon monoxide which can be lethal. Ensure that the house has smoke detectors and a carbon monoxide alarm.

Check that the windows fit and shut properly. Check for electricity sockets in all rooms. Overloading a single socket with extra extensions can be a potential fire hazard. Check the furniture for British Safety Standard stickers for fire resistance. Remember, if there are night storage heaters or electric bar fires as the main source of heating, this will triple your bills. Check how far the house is from your university or college and what forms of public transport are available for you to commute.

Security
Thieves often target student houses, so check how secure the house is:

◆ Check whether the external doors have secure deadlocks or just a standard lock.

◆ Check whether the windows have key operated locks.

◆ Check whether there are any other doors that provide easy access for thieves, for example back doors or kitchen doors.

◆ Check whether anyone other than the tenant/s has a key to the house. If you have a shared tenancy, only the tenants are entitled to a key.

- Check how good the outside and the backyard lighting is. Good lighting often deters thieves at night.

- Take out insurance on your possessions/home contents.

Contracts

Before you sign a contract think about whether you want to sign joint or individual contracts (see below), and discuss this amongst yourselves and with the landlord. Don't sign anything before you have had it checked by the housing advice service, your Student Advice Centre or Citizens Advice Bureau.

Joint versus individual

- On a joint contract you are all liable for all the rent (not just your own share) and bills. On an individual contract you are only liable for your own rent and bills.

- On a joint contract you help to decide in who moves into your house. On individual contracts the landlord can choose.

- On a joint contract you are all liable for any council tax there may be. On individual contracts the landlord is liable.

- On a joint contract the landlord does not have the right to come into your home without your prior knowledge. On an individual contract the landlord can come into the communal areas whenever she or he wants to but can only come into your room with your prior knowledge.

Most contracts run for a fixed term, usually one year. Get a break clause written in. This allows you to give notice before the fixed term is finished and terminate the contract. The wording for a break clause is legally technical. Your student accommodation office, housing advice centre and the Student Advice Centre will have copies of the correct wording. Check when the rent is payable – weekly or monthly. If the landlord asks for post-dated cheques, try to argue against them. In the UK post-dated cheques can be cashed at any time, not just after the date written on them. Try to avoid paying in cash. If the landlord insists on cash payments make sure you get a receipt for every payment. Check who is responsible for water rates and have it written into the contract.

As a full-time student you are exempt from paying council tax. But remember, only houses where all the tenants are students are exempt from council tax. If you will be sharing with other non-students, then you'll be liable for payment.

If the landlord agrees to any necessary repairs, supplying more furniture or decorating before you move in, make sure it is written into the contract with a completion date. Remember, once you have signed the contract all that is written is legally binding. Be aware of what you are signing. Get it checked first with your local housing advice centre, Citizens Advice Bureau or your Student Advice Centre. If you have signed a joint contract then remember to keep a photocopy of the contract for your records.

IMPORTANT

- Don't give anybody any money before signing the contract.

- Don't sign the contract until you have had it checked by the local housing advice service, your Student Advice Centre or Citizens Advice Bureau. A contract is a legally binding document and by signing it you are committing yourself to those terms for one year or more.

Deposits

Landlords usually ask for a deposit. A deposit is an amount of money (usually the equivalent of one month's rent) paid to the landlord at the start of the tenancy. It is security against any damage you might do to the house or the fixtures and fittings during your tenancy.

Get the deposit amount written into the contract and the date on which it will be returned – usually within 14 days of the end of the tenancy. Legally, deposits cannot be used in lieu of rent – if a landlord says she or he will keep your deposit in lieu of the last month's rent, get her or him to sign a piece of paper to that effect.

Housemates

One of the problems you could encounter once you move into your house may be to do with the people with whom you are sharing. However great they may be as friends, they may not be so great as housemates. Little things that initially may annoy can turn into major issues over a period of 12 months. To make sharing a house with other people work, there will inevitably have to be compromise and negotiation. Things like cleaning the kitchen may seem like minor issues, but if you end up being the only person doing it, resentment may well ensue. Talk about cleaning and tidying issues. Also bear in mind that partners of your house-mates could easily become permanent fixtures in the house. While you are studying you do not need the added pressure of squabbles at home. And, of course, if you and your house-mates all get on well, any major issues that come up will be easier to deal with.

Moving in

Before you move in you will need to do an inventory of the property. It is best to do a very thorough inventory so make a note of every plate and cup, every chip in the paintwork, every tear in the wallpaper, every mark on the carpet etc. If possible, take a camera with you and photograph the property. Although most landlords are trustworthy, there are always some who will try to keep your deposit because of 'damages'. If you have photographs of the property as it was when you moved in then you will have evidence to back up your case if she or he does not return your deposit. This is time-consuming, but worth doing if you want to get your money back. Make sure the photographs are signed by yourselves and the landlord.

Utility bills (water, electricity, gas and telephone)

Check all the meters when you move in (water (if applicable), gas and electricity). When you contact the utility companies, spread the responsibility amongst yourselves. Do not put all the bills in one person's name. The person named on the bill will be the person pursued for payment. There are several private utility providers in the UK and the prices for their services vary. Compare the costs of utility companies by checking online at www.uswitch.com

Major telephone companies in the UK are British Telecommunications (BT) and NTL. If the property that you are moving into has never had a telephone line then you will need a new line installed. Monthly rental for a standard telephone line starts from £9. You can contact BT (www.bt.com) on 0800 800 150 or NTL (www.ntl.com) on 0800 183 0123.

Council tax

Council tax is a charge made by the local authority on properties within the borough. Each property falls within a valuation band and the council tax bill is decided according to the valuation band the property is in. Council tax rates change annually and the year runs from 1 April.

Council tax exemption certificates

Students have to prove their full-time status and the university or college is obliged to issue a certificate confirming this, including the dates and the length of the course. Your college administrator or your university's academic registrar's office will issue these certificates. Keep this certificate safe.

The dependent or spouse of an international student will not have to pay council tax if they are not EEA citizens. International spouses who are allowed to work will not have to pay council tax as the terms of their visa state that they can have no recourse to public funds. This means that they will be exempt from council tax, as long as there are no other liable people living in the property.

You will need to get your council tax exemption certificate and send this to the council soon after you move in. The person named on the contract will be the one pursued for the payment of council tax, and it is your responsibility to make sure the council knows that you live in a student-only house and are therefore exempt. If you have non-students living in the property, the students will still need to provide their exemption certificates. If you are living with non-students, discuss with them who is going to pay what share of the council tax liability. If you move in with students and then somebody leaves university or college before the end of their course, the council will need to be informed and there could be financial implications. Talk about it sooner rather than later.

Housing advice service

This is an independent service provided by local councils for the benefit of tenants and landlords. They should be your first point of contact if you run into difficulties. They can be reached by telephone or in person. Check the local telephone directory for their number and location.

REPAIRS AND MAINTENANCE

Landlord's responsibility

The basic rule of thumb for repairs is that if you break it, you fix it. If something breaks down because it's old and hasn't been repaired in years, then it is probably the landlord's responsibility. Although the landlord does have to ensure that you have hot water and heating, if the water pipes burst over the winter because you did not put the heating on, then again it is your responsibility. If you go home over Christmas, the best rule is to leave the heating on all the time at about 10°C, so that the pipes will not freeze.

Your landlord has various legal responsibilities. These include meeting all health and safety standards as required by British law; maintaining the structure of the building; maintaining all fixtures and fittings. It is his or her responsibility to keep in repair and proper working order the installations for the supply of water, gas and electricity and all sanitation. If, as part of the tenancy agreement, you have rented from her or him a TV, cooker, washing machine etc. then she or he has a duty to ensure that these are in good working order. If anything goes wrong with the above, he or she should repair it within 48 hours. Phone the landlord and tell her or him, and follow it up with a letter. Keep copies of all correspondence with the landlord regarding any repairs.

When things go wrong, give your landlord a reasonable amount of time (around 14–21 days) for the work to be done. If the repairs are not done, contact the housing advice centre, Citizens Advice Bureau or your Student Advice Centre for further advice. Do not withhold rent. It is illegal and the landlord could have you evicted from the property.

Tenant's responsibility

As a tenant you have certain responsibilities. You are responsible for repairs to anything you break, and this will include any fixtures and fittings broken because of your actions.

It is your responsibility to keep any sinks and toilets unblocked, to turn off the water when you go away, to keep the house and its contents clean, to take all possible action to keep the pipes from freezing in winter and to notify the landlord of all necessary repairs as soon as possible.

In your contract there will be a 'noise clause'. This is a fairly new amendment to the law, and can potentially cause problems. Befriend your neighbours quickly, because if they complain and it is upheld in court, you could be left homeless almost immediately. Your neighbours are entitled to quiet and peaceful enjoyment of their property.

Harassment

The landlord has restricted access to your home during your tenancy, and you have the legal right to a quiet and peaceful enjoyment of the property. You are entitled to 'peacefully hold and enjoy the premises during the tenancy without any interruption by the landlord or his agent'. This means the landlord cannot be constantly popping in and telling you what to do. Nor can she or he come round to threaten you.

A landlord must give 24 hours' notice if she or he wishes to visit the property for a valid reason, e.g. repairs, once every three or four months to check it over or to show new tenants around. If it is a shared tenancy the landlord does not have a right to the keys and you can change the locks. If you have a single or individual contract the landlord has a right to hold the keys to the main doors but not your individual bedrooms.

Moving out

If you want to move out before your contract expires, seek advice from the housing advice centre or your Student Advice Centre. Give notice to your landlord, even on a fixed term contract, to enable your landlord to get the deposit organised. Tidy and clean the house and, with the landlord, go through the exit inventory. Again, remember to get the inventory signed by both parties and take photos as proof as necessary. Do not forget to inform the utility companies that you are leaving the property and take meter readings. Lastly, leave a forwarding address with the landlord or new tenants and make arrangements for your mail to be forwarded with the Royal Mail.

GLOSSARY OF ACCOMMODATION TERMS

Break clause: A clause that permits a tenant or landlord to end a tenancy agreement at a particular period of time during the tenancy.

Contract: A legally binding agreement between two parties.

CORGI (Council for Registered Gas Installers): CORGI is the national supervisory body for gas safety in the UK.

Council tax: A local tax on all properties within the borough. Each property falls within a valuation band and the council tax bill is decided according to the valuation band the property is in and the number of people living in it. Council tax rates change annually and the year runs from 1 April.

Damp: Mainly caused by condensation inside the house. Damp inside the house encourages the growth of moulds and mites which can cause severe respiratory problems.

Deposit: A sum of money held as a security for a period of time. The deposit may be repaid with or without interest.

Gas certificate: A certificate that guarantees that all gas-operated appliances and the gas supply in the house are safe. The certificate is issued after checks carried out by a CORGI registered installer. The certificate is valid for a year.

Rent: A regular payment by a tenant to a landlord for use of the property over a period of time. This can be weekly, monthly or quarterly.

USEFUL WEBSITES

www.hostuk.org

The Host UK website has complete information on host availability, locations, the application process, and general information for students wishing to live with a host family.

www.adviceguide.org.uk
The website of the Citizens Advice Bureau has a section devoted completely to housing advice. The site has a search facility where you can get further details on local housing advice in your area.

www.accommodationsforstudents.com
A privately operated website that has details of properties available in the major university towns and cities in the UK. The site has student reviews on shops, transport and other facilities within each locality for every town.

www.netlet.co.uk
This is a private website that advertises accommodation for students in London, Brighton, Cranfield, Leeds, Bradford and Bretton. The website also has a student-to-student notice-board which allows students to communicate with other students with similar backgrounds and requirements e.g. ethnic groupings and language requirements. There is also a section on short let for students wanting to leave and those wanting to find replacement flatmates.

www.corgi-gas-safety.com
The website of the gas regulatory body of the UK. The site offers a search facility for local CORGI registered installers as well as useful information on gas safety and the law.

www.odpm.gov.uk
The website of the Deputy Prime Minister's Office that has several downloadable booklets for advice on renting houses in the UK.

www.direct.gov.uk

A government-run website that has a section on house renting. The site also offers advice on problems usually associated with tenants and landlords.

www.energywatch.org.uk

Energywatch is the supervisory body for all gas and electricity companies in the UK. The website provides free and impartial advice to consumers on a wide range of issues including making savings on gas and electricity bills. The website also has a complaints facility for problems related to energy suppliers.

www.uswitch.com

An independent website that compares the prices of all utility services in your area. The website also provides you with the best prices, special offers and services from every utility supplier.

www.shelter.org.uk

Shelter is a non-profit organisation that advises on housing issues. The website has a series of downloadable booklets giving detailed information and advice on a range of housing issues.

www.studentpad.co.uk

Another privately operated website that offers search facilities for student accommodation in all major university towns and cities.

www.ukpropertyshop.co.uk

This is the website of the National Association of Letting Agents. The national directory has a search facility for all letting agents and links to their own websites in your locality.

10

What Next?

Your fruitful stay as a student in Britain would not be fully so without a proper ending! In other words, make sure you deal with little matters that need to be attended to after you have completed your course. Almost all of you will be considering your career ahead, but there may be other things that need to be handled and dealt with before you can progress. Some of these could be financial, like having to pay back your debts, cancel your credit cards, close your bank accounts or terminate your lease. Some of these could be legal, like having to find a way to prolong your stay in Britain. Others could be logistical, like sending your belongings back home. Some could be emotional matters, like having to say goodbye to your college and go back to your country: a sorrowful task for many. Some of you may want to stay back for a second course and may wonder how to do that.

You will have to say goodbye to many of your friends and
teachers. After an international programme your classmates could
disperse all over the world. Make sure you keep their postal
addresses, email addresses, and phone numbers. You never know
when you will need them. Keep contact details for your
instructors and professors. Try to collect letters of
recommendation from your favourite instructors. If you are
leaving the country for good, collect as many photographs as
possible to help you remember your stay.

APPLYING FOR ANOTHER COURSE

If you wish to stay on for another course follow the application
procedure given in Chapter 1 of this book. If you are a non-EEA
national then you will have to extend your visa by filling in a
standard application form available from your International
Office, your Student Advice Centre or directly from the Home
Office website at www.ind.homeoffice.gov.uk and apply to the
Home Office. Check further immigration details in Chapter 4.

STAYING ON AS A TOURIST OR FOR GRADUATION

Non-EEA students who have completed their degree course are
allowed to stay on for another six months as a tourist. You may
have to get an extension on your permission to stay by filling in a
standard application form available from your International
Office, your Student Advice Centre or directly from the Home
Office website at www.ind.homeoffice.gov.uk and apply to the
Home Office. Check further immigration details in Chapter 4.

WORKING IN THE UK AFTER YOUR STUDIES

Lots of companies in the UK recruit graduates directly from
universities. For detailed lists of graduate jobs see:

- Prospects (www.prospects.ac.uk)
- Jobs (www.jobs.ac.uk)
- Gradunet (www.gradunet.co.uk).

Several companies advertise graduate jobs in the local and national media, and attend careers fairs held annually in every college and university. Your university's careers advisory service will also have a detailed list of all graduate jobs in the locality and will also help you fill in an application forms and to prepare for interviews.

EEA nationals

As an EEA national, you are permitted to work freely in the UK and may find employment easily. There are no restrictions on your stay in the UK and you can engage in any form of work or business.

Non-EEA nationals and work permits

Although non-EEA students are not required to have a work permit whilst studying full-time in the UK, they will need to get one if they decide to pursue employment in the UK. It has often been difficult for overseas students to obtain work permits after studying in the UK. Previous regulations did not permit non-EEA students to stay in the UK while applying for a permit to work. However, these regulations are being changed, making it easier for students to apply for work permits after finishing their course. Work permits have to be applied for on behalf of the student by their employer and a decision is usually made on the application within a fortnight. Your Student Advice Centre, International Office or your local Citizens Advice Bureau can provide further information about this. Alternatively you can check directly online at www.workingintheuk.gov.uk

Highly skilled migrant programme

The British government has introduced a points-based migrant system, similar to those in Australia and Canada, to encourage highly skilled people to seek work or self employment opportunities in the UK. This scheme is slightly different from work permits as you do not have to have a job offer in order to apply. You can apply for it within the UK. Your Student Advice Centre, International Office or your local Citizens Advice Bureau can provide further information on this. Alternatively you can check directly at www.hsmp-services.co.uk

STUDENTS IN SCOTLAND

Due to a decline in birth rates in Scotland, non-EEA international students studying in Scotland are being encouraged to stay and find work in Scotland. Currently, international students who have graduated with a degree from a Scottish university are being permitted to stay in Scotland for an additional two years without having to obtain a work permit. Students in Scotland should contact their Student Advice Centre, International Office or their local Citizens Advice Bureau for further information on this. The website www.scotlandistheplace.co.uk has further details about this programme.

STORAGE

During vacations, or a temporary visit abroad, you may have to or want to vacate your halls of residence and go home for a short break. There are lots of private companies offering secure storage facilities to students from around £5 per week. Companies that have branches in the UK are:

- Shurguard (www.shurguard.co.uk)
- Big Yellow Storage (www.bigyellow.co.uk or 0800 783 4949)

- ◆ Safe Store (www.safestore.co.uk)
- ◆ Avk storage (www.avk.co.uk).

Several other local companies are listed in *Yellow Pages.*

SENDING GOODS BACK HOME

During your stay in the UK as a student you'll probably have accumulated quite a lot of stuff that you might want to take back home. Most airlines limit the amount of luggage you can take with you on the flight (usually around 20 kilos for an economy ticket or two pieces of luggage to the United States). You will probably be better off shipping the items home as airlines will not permit you to take them with you as luggage or will charge you extra (around 2 per cent of the full fare per kilo).

Sending goods back home by airfreight is a lot quicker than using a haulage company but it is expensive because airfreight companies charge you according to weight. On the other hand, shipping companies charge according to size and this can work out a lot cheaper. However, they are slow and you should expect it to take around three to four weeks for goods to arrive back in the US by ship. Most of these companies offer free collection. Remember it is worth insuring your goods before shipping them in case they are damaged during transit. Also, do make sure that the company you choose are listed with BAR (British Association of Removers). The Excess Baggage Company (www.excess-baggage.com or 0800 783 1085) has branches at all major airports and offers a collection service from major towns in the UK. They charge around £5 per kilo with a minimum weight of 25 kilos plus a £30 handling fee. Atlantis Overseas Removals (www.atlantisltd. co.uk or 0121 451 1588) is another company that has branches all

around the UK. Several other freight companies are listed in
Yellow Pages. Your International Office or your Student Advice
Centre will also have list of all locally available freight companies.

Taking money back home

The easiest and the safest way to take money back home would be
to arrange a bank transfer to your home bank account. Bank
transfers take around three to four days and cost around £10–£15.
You could also buy travellers' cheques or a banker's draft in your
preferred currency as a safe and cheap method of taking money
back home in person. You can also send money electronically to a
recipient in your home country using Western Union or
Moneygram. Charges for these are higher than those for the other
methods.

Buying goods to take home

Gifts or souvenirs

Almost every town has a gift shop selling uniquely designed gifts
relating to the region or local football clubs. These can be t-shirts,
mugs, pens, tea-towels, picture frames, local delicacies, coasters
etc. Universities and Students' Union shops also sell their own
crested clothing and other souvenirs. Reserve one early as they
usually sell out quickly at the end of term.

Other items

If you intend to buy any electrical items make sure they are
adaptable for use in your country. If you are flying out of the
European Union then it might be worth buying some items such
as spirits, perfumes and tobacco at the airport duty-free shops
rather than in a supermarket or off-licence as these are highly
taxed items in the UK. If you are a non-EEA National or a

resident leaving the EEA territory, and these goods are taken or sent home you may be able to get back the VAT (Value Added Tax) if you buy them within three months of leaving the UK. You'll need to ask the dealer for a VAT refund certificate (Form704/1) at the time of purchase and produce your non-EEA passport. Contact the International Office or your Student Advice Centre for information on how to best go about this. VAT refund details are also available on the web at www.hmrc.gov.uk Before taking goods home, check the customs regulations in your home country as some items may be prohibited or incur a customs duty.

Checklist before you go home

1. **Closing bank accounts**

   If you are leaving the UK permanently then notify the bank, withdraw your cash and transfer it back home. If you are planning to come back to the UK after some time then it may be worthwhile to keep the account open with a minimal deposit in it.

2. **Closing other accounts (mobile, telephone, gas, electricity, etc.)**

   Do not forget to inform any other companies that you have a contract with and close your accounts with them. Also check whether you owe them money or are owed money by them.

3. **Sending money back home**

   Do not send large sums of money back home by post as it is not safe and might violate customs regulations in your country. Try taking it back or sending it using the methods listed above.

4. **Book your flights/train/ferry/bus early**

   Transport usually gets booked up quickly during July, September and December – the time when most overseas students go back home. Booking early will enable you to get a less expensive ticket and will help you to plan your return journey with ease.

5. **Tax refund**

   If you have been working in the UK and think you have earned well below the income tax threshold then you might be eligible for a tax refund. Contact your Student Advice Centre, International Office or your local Citizens Advice Bureau for further details on getting a tax refund.

6. **Check customs regulations in your country**

   Before buying goods to take back home check the customs regulations in your country as some items may be prohibited or incur a customs duty.

7. **Shopping for souvenirs or gifts**

   Do not forget to buy souvenirs or gifts from the UK for your friends and family at home.

8. **VAT refunds**

   To claim you must buy goods which you are taking back home three months before you leave the UK. You'll need to ask the dealer for a VAT refund certificate (Form 704/1) at the time of purchase and produce your non-EEA passport.

9. **Collecting references**

   Do not forget to collect references from your supervisors and other academics as they will be useful back home.

10. **Joining alumni**

    By joining the alumni you can maintain your links with your educational institution in the UK. The alumni also helps you to keep in touch with your old classmates. There is usually a small fee for joining the alumni.

11. **Leaving a forwarding address**

    Do not forget to leave a forwarding address with your educational institution, landlord and any other parties concerned. This will also help you to get your mail redirected to your place of residence.

Selling your things

If you have things that you do not want to take back home then try to sell them well before you leave the UK (around one–two months). Try advertising textbooks in the Students' Union, the institution's online bulletin boards and departmental notice-boards. You can also try selling them to local second-hand book shops, book shops on campus or on Amazon (www.amazon.co.uk) and ebay (www.ebay.co.uk). You may be able to charge up to 70 per cent of the cost price depending on the quality of your textbook. Other goods can also be advertised in the Students' Union, departmental notice-boards, the institution's online bulletin boards as well as in shop windows around town.

Donating your things

You might like to consider donating your unwanted items to local charity shops. (You will probably know where these are located in your town by the end of your stay in the UK!) You may also want to consider passing on some items to your friends if they are staying on in the UK.

REVERSE CULTURE SHOCK

When you return home at the end of your studies, you may experience feelings of disorientation which may surprise you, as you expect home to be a familiar place. However, your family, friends, colleagues and your country are likely to have changed even in a year. Colleges and universities usually offer a short course in the spring or summer term to assist students returning home to acclimatise.

USEFUL WEBSITES

www.workingintheuk.gov.uk

This government-run website has complete details about working in the UK, work permits and the application process.

www.scotlandistheplace.co.uk

For students in Scotland, this website gives information on the new government programme to encourage international students to stay in the UK for up to two years after their graduation

www.hsmp-services.co.uk

This website provides full details of the Highly Skilled Migrant Programme of the UK including the points calculator, application and other details.

www.ukcosa.org.uk

UK Council for Overseas Students Affairs has further guidance and advice on preparing to go home.

www.hmrc.gov.uk

The website for Customs and Excise has complete details on VAT refunds and how to apply for a VAT refund before your departure from the UK.

ALDERMOOR FARM

Appendix –
British Universities and Colleges

University of Aberdeen
King's College
Aberdeen AB24 3FX
Tel: 01224 272 000
Fax: 01224 488 611
www.aberdeen.ac.uk

University of Abertay, Dundee
Bell Street
Dundee
Tel: 01382 308 000
Fax: 01382 308 877
www.abertay.ac.uk

Anglia Polytechnic University
Victoria Road South
Chelmsford CM1 1LL
Tel: 01245 493 131
Fax: 01245 490 835
www.apu.ac.uk

Aston University
Aston Triangle
Birmingham B4 7ET
Tel: 0121 204 3000
Fax: 0121 333 6350
www.aston.ac.uk

University of Bath
Claverton Down
Bath BA2 7AY
Tel: 01225 826 826
Fax: 01225 462 508
www.bath.ac.uk

Queens University of Belfast
University Road
Belfast BT7 1NN
Tel: 02890 245 133
Fax: 02890 975 137
www.qub.ac.uk

University of Birmingham
Edgbaston
Birmingham B15 2TT
Tel: 0121 414 3344
Fax: 0121 414 3971
www.birmingham.ac.uk

University of Central England in Birmingham
Perry Barr
Birmingham B42 2SU
Tel: 0121 331 5595
Fax: 0121 331 7994
www.uce.ac.uk

University of Bolton
Deane Road
Bolton BL3 5AB
Tel: 01204 528 851
Fax: 01204 399 074
www.bolton.ac.uk

Bournemouth University
Fern Barrow
Poole
Dorset BH12 5BB
Tel: 01202 524 111
Fax: 01202 962 736
www.bournemouth.ac.uk

University of Bradford
Richmond Road
Bradford BD7 1DP
Tel: 01274 232 323
Fax: 01274 235 953
www.bradford.ac.uk

University of Brighton
Mithras House
Lewes Road
Brighton BN2 4AT
Tel: 01273 600 900
Fax: 01273 642 825
www.brighton.ac.uk

University of Bristol
Senate House
Tyndall Avenue
Bristol BS8 1TH
Tel: 0117 928 9000
Fax: 0117 925 1424
www.bristol.ac.uk

University of West England, Bristol
Frenchay Campus
Coldharbour Lane

Bristol BS16 1QY
Tel: 0117 965 6261
Fax: 0117 976 3804
www.uwe.ac.uk

Brunel University
Uxbridge
Middlesex UB8 3PH
Tel: 01895 274 4000
Fax: 01895 232 806
www.brunel.ac.uk

University of Buckingham
Hunter Street
Buckingham MK18 1EG
Tel: 01280 814 080
Fax: 01280 822 245
www.buckingham.ac.uk

University of Cambridge
University Registry
The Old Schools
Cambridge CB2 1TN
Tel: 01223 337 733
Fax: 01233 332 332
www.cam.ac.uk

City University
Northampton Square
London EC1V OHB
Tel: 020 7040 5060
Fax: 020 7040 5070
www.city.ac.uk

Coventry University
Priory Street
Coventry CV1 5FB
Tel: 024 7688 7688
Fax: 024 7688 8793
www.coventry.ac.uk

Cranfield University
Cranfield
Bedfordshire MK43 0AL
Tel: 01234 750 111
Fax: 01234 750 875
www.cranfield.ac.uk

De Montfort University
Leicester Campus
The Gateway
Leicester LE1 9BH
Tel: 0116 255 1551
Fax: 0116 255 1551
www.demontfort.ac.uk

Bedford Campus
37 Landsdowne Road
Bedford MK40 2BZ
Tel: 01234 351 966
Fax: 01234350 833
www.dmu.ac.uk

Lincoln Campus
Caythorpe Court
Caythorpe
Grantham NG32 3EP

Tel: 01522 512 912
Fax: 01400 272 722
www.dmu.ac.uk

Milton Keynes Campus
Kents Hill
Hammerwood Gate
Milton Keynes MK7 6HP
Tel: 01905 695 511
Fax: 01905 695 581
www.dmu.ac.uk

University of Derby
Kedleston Road
Derby DE22 1GB
Tel: 01332 590 500
Fax: 01322 294 861
www.derby.ac.uk

University of Dundee
Nethergate
Dundee DD1 4HN
Tel: 01382 344 000
Fax: 01382 201 604
www.dundee.ac.uk

University of Durham
Old Shire Hall
Old Elvet
Durham DH1 3HP
Tel: 0191 334 2000
Fax: 0191 334 6326
www.durham.ac.uk

University of East Anglia
Norwich NR4 7TJ
Tel: 01603 456 161
Fax: 01603 458 553
www.uea.ac.uk

University of East London
Barking Campus
Long Bridge Road
Dagenham RM8 2AS
Tel: 020 8223 3000
Fax: 020 8590 7799
www.uel.ac.uk

Stratford Campus
Romford Road
London E15 4LZ
Tel: 020 8223 3000
Fax: 020 8590 7799
www.uel.ac.uk

University of Edinburgh
Old College
South Bridge
Edinburgh EH8 9YL
Tel: 0131 650 1000
Fax: 0131 650 8223
www.edinburgh.ac.uk

University of Essex
Wivenhoe Park
Colchester CO4 3SQ
Tel: 01206 873 333
Fax: 01206 873 410
www.essex.ac.uk

University of Exeter
Northcote House
The Queens Drive
Exeter EX4 4QJ
Tel: 01392 661 000
Fax: 01392 263 108
www.exeter.ac.uk

University of Glamorgan
Pontypridd
Mid Glamorgan
Glamorgan CF37 1DL
Tel: 01433 480 480
Fax: 01433 480 0558
www.glam.ac.uk

University of Glasgow
Glasgow G12 8QQ
Tel: 0141 330 2000
Fax: 0141 330 4413
www.glasgow.ac.uk

Glasgow Caledonian University
70 Cowcaddens Road
Glasgow G4 OBA
Tel: 0141 331 3000
Fax: 0141 331 3005
www.gcal.ac.uk

University of Greenwich
Maritime Greenwich Campus
Old Royal Naval College
Park Row, Greenwich

London SE10 9LS
Tel: 020 8331 8000
Fax: 020 8331 8145
www.greenwich.ac.uk

Heriot-Watt University
Riccarton
Edinburgh EH14 4AS
Tel: 0131 449 5111
Fax: 0131 449 5153
www.heriot-watt.ac.uk

University of Hertfordshire
College Lane
Hatfield AL10 9AB
Tel: 01707 284 000
Fax: 01707 284 870
www.herts.ac.uk

University of Huddersfield
Queens Gate
Huddersfield HD1 3DH
Tel: 01484 4222 288
Fax: 01484 516 151
www.hud.ac.uk

University of Hull
Cottingham Road
Hull HU6 7RX
Tel: 01482 346 311
Fax: 01482 469 536
www.hull.ac.uk

Keele University
Keele ST5 5BG
Tel: 01782 621 111
Fax: 01782 632 343
www.keele.ac.uk

University of Kent
Canterbury CT2 7NZ
Tel: 01227 764 000
Fax: 01227 452 196
www.kent.ac.uk

Kingston University
53-57 High Street
Kingston-upon-Thames KT1 1LQ
Tel: 020 8547 2000
Fax: 020 8547 7859
www.kingston.ac.uk

University of Central Lancashire
Corporation Street
Preston PR1 2HE
Tel: 01772 201 201
Fax: 01772 892 935
www.uclan.ac.uk

Lancaster University
Bailrigg
Lancaster LA1 4YW
Tel: 01524 652 01
Fax: 01524 63806
www.lancaster.ac.uk

University of Leeds
Woodhouse Lane
Leeds LS2 9JT
Tel: 0113 243 1751
Fax: 0113 244 3923
www.leeds.ac.uk

Leeds Metropolitan University
Calverley Street
Leeds LS1 3HE
Tel: 0113 283 2600
Fax: 0113 283 3114
www.lmu.ac.uk

University of Leicester
University Road
Leicester LE1 7RH
Tel: 0116 252 2522
Fax: 0116 252 2200
www.leicester.ac.uk

University of Liverpool
Abercromby Square
PO Box 147
Liverpool L69 3BX
Tel: 0151 794 2000
Fax: 0151 708 6502
www.liverpool.ac.uk

Liverpool Hope University
Hope Park
Liverpool L16 9JD
Tel: 0151 291 3000

Fax: 0151 291 3444
www.hope.ac.uk

Liverpool John Moores University
Roscoe House
4 Rodney Street
Liverpool L3 5UX
Tel: 0151 231 5090
Fax: 0151 231 3194
www.livjm.ac.uk

University of the Arts
65 Davies Street
London W1K 5DA
Tel: 0207 514 6000
Fax: 0207 514 6131
www.arts.ac.uk

University of London
Malet Street
London WC1E 7HU
Tel: 020 7862 8000
Fax: 020 7636 5875
www.london.ac.uk

London Metropolitan University
31 Jewry Street
London EC3N 2EY
Tel: 020 7423 0000
Fax: 020 7133 2240
www.londonmet.ac.uk

Loughborough University
Ashby Road
Loughborough LE11 3TU
Tel: 01509 263 171
Fax: 0509 265 687
www.loughborough.ac.uk

University of Luton
Park Square
Luton LU1 3JU
Tel: 01582 34111
Fax: 01582 489 323
www.luton.ac.uk

University of Manchester
Oxford Road
Manchester M13 9PL
Tel: 0161 306 6000
Fax: 0161 275 2058
www.manchester.ac.uk

Manchester Business School
Booth Street West
Manchester M13 9PL
Tel: 0161 275 6303
Fax: 0161 275 6304
www.mbs.ac.uk

Manchester Metropolitan University
All Saints Building
All Saints
Manchester M15 6BH
Tel: 0161 247 2000

Fax: 0161 247 6390
www.mmu.ac.uk

Middlesex University
North London Business Park
Oakleigh Road South
London N11 1QS
Tel: 020 8411 5000
Fax: 020 8362 6878
www.middlesex.ac.uk

Napier University
219 Colinton Road
Edinburgh EH14 1DJ
Tel: 0131 455 6331
Fax: 0131 455 6334
www.napier.ac.uk

University of Newcastle upon Tyne
6–10 Kensington Terrace
Newcastle NE1 7RU
Tel: 0191 222 6138
Fax: 0191 222 6139
www.newcastle.ac.uk

University of Northumbria at Newcastle
Ellison Place
Newcastle NE1 8ST
Tel: 0191 232 6002
Fax: 0191 227 4017
www.northumbria.ac.uk

University of Nottingham
University Park
Nottingham NG7 2RD
Tel: 0115 951 5151
Fax: 0115 951 3666
www.nottingham.ac.uk

Nottingham Trent University
Burton Street
Nottingham NG1 4BU
Tel: 0115 941 8418
Fax: 0115 948 6063
www.ntu.ac.uk

University of Oxford
Wellington Square
Oxford OX1 2JD
Tel: 01865 270 000
Fax: 01865 270 708
www.oxford.ac.uk

Oxford Brookes University
Gipsy Lane
Headington
Oxford OX3 OBP
Tel: 01865 741 111
Fax: 01865 483 983
www.brookes.ac.uk

University of Paisley
High Street
Paisley PA1 2BE
Tel: 0141 848 3000

Fax: 0141 848 3682
www.paisley.ac.uk

University of Plymouth
Drake Circus
Plymouth PL4 8AA
Tel: 01752 600 600
Fax: 01752 232 141
www.plymouth.ac.uk

University of Portsmouth
Winston Churchill Avenue
Portsmouth PO1 2UP
Tel: 02392 84 84 84
Fax: 02392 84 30 82
www.portsmouth.ac.uk

University of Reading
Whiteknights
PO Box 217
Reading RG6 6AH
Tel: 0118 987 5123
Fax: 0118 931 4404
www.reading.ac.uk

Robert Gordon University
School Hill
Aberdeen AB19 1FR
Tel: 01224 262 000
Fax: 01224 263 000
www.rgu.ac.uk

University of St Andrews
College Gate
St Andrews KY16 9AJ
Tel: 01334 476 161
Fax: 01344 473 388
www.st-andrews.ac.uk

University of Salford
Salford M5 4WT
Tel: 0161 295 5000
Fax: 0161 295 5999
www.salford.ac.uk

University of Sheffield
Sheffield S10 2TN
Tel: 0114 222 2000
Fax: 0114 273 9826
www.sheffield.ac.uk

Sheffield Hallam University
Howard Street
Sheffield S1 1WB
Tel: 0114 225 5555
Fax: 0114 225 2094
www.shu.ac.uk

South Bank University
103 Borough Road
London SE1 0AA
Tel: 020 7928 8989
Fax: 020 7815 8273
www.lsbu.ac.uk

University of Southampton
University Road
Highfield
Southampton S10 2TN
Tel: 023 8059 5000
Fax: 023 8059 3939
www.southampton.ac.uk

Staffordshire University
College Road
Stoke-on-Trent ST4 2DE
Tel: 01782 294 000
Fax: 01782 745 422
www.staffs.ac.uk

University of Stirling
Stirling FK9 4LA
Tel: 01786 473 171
Fax: 01786 466 800
www.stir.ac.uk

University of Strathclyde
McCance Building
16 Richmond Street
Glasgow G1 1XQ
Tel: 0141 552 4400
Fax: 0141 552 5860
www.strath.ac.uk

University of Sunderland
Chester Road
Sunderland SR2 7PS
Tel: 0191 515 2000

Fax: 0191 510 2203
www.sunderland.ac.uk

University of Surrey
Guildford GU2 7XH
Tel: 01483 300 800
Fax: 01483 300 803
www.surrey.ac.uk

University of Sussex
Sussex House
Brighton BN1 9RH
Tel: 01273 606 755
Fax: 01273 678 335
www.sussex.ac.uk

University of Teesside
Borough Road
Middlesborough TS1 3BA
Tel: 01642 218 121
Fax: 01642 342 067
www.tees.ac.uk

Thames Valley University
St Mary's Road
Ealing
London W5 5RF
Tel: 020 8579 5000
Fax: 020 8231 2900
www.tvu.ac.uk

University of Ulster
Cromore Road

Coleraine BT52 1SA
Tel: 02870 324 138
Fax: 02870 324 930
www.ulster.ac.uk

University of Wales, Aberystwyth
Kings Street
Aberystwyth SY23 2AX
Tel: 01970 623 111
Fax: 01970 622 063
www.aber.ac.uk

University of Wales, Bangor
Bangor SY23 2AX
Tel: 01248 351 151
Fax: 01248 382 015
www.bangor.ac.uk

University of Wales, Cardiff
Cardiff CF10 3XQ
Tel: 029 2087 4000
Fax: 029 2087 4622
www.cardiff.ac.uk

University of Wales, Lampeter
Lampeter SA48 7ED
Tel: 01570 422 351
Fax: 01570 423 423
www.lamp.ac.uk

University of Wales, Swansea
Singleton Park
Swansea SA2 8PP

Tel: 01792 205 678
Fax: 01792 295 157
www.swan.ac.uk

University of Warwick
Gibbet Hill Road
Coventry CV4 7AL
Tel: 024 7652 3523
Fax: 024 7646 1606
www.warwick.ac.uk

University of Westminster
309 Regent Street
London W1B 2UW
Tel: 020 7911 5000
Fax: 020 7911 5858
www.westminster.ac.uk

The University of Winchester
Sparkford Road
Winchester SO22 4NR
Tel: 01962 841 515
Fax: 01962 842 280
www.winchester.ac.uk

University of Wolverhampton
Wulfruna Street
Wolverhampton WV1 1SB
Tel: 01902 321 000
Fax: 01902 322 528
www.wlv.ac.uk

University of York
Heslington
York YO1 5DD
Tel: 01904 430 000
Fax: 01904 433 433
www.york.ac.uk

Colleges affiliated to University of London
Birkbeck College
Malet Street
Bloomsbury
London WC1E 7HX
Tel: 020 7631 6000
Fax: 020 7631 6270
www.birkbeck.ac.uk

Goldsmiths College
New Cross
London SE14 6NW
Tel: 020 7919 7171
Fax: 020 7919 7704
www.goldsmiths.ac.uk

Imperial College
South Kensington
London SW7 2AZ
Tel: 020 7589 5111
Fax: 020 7591 8004
www.imperial.ac.uk

Kings College
Strand
London WC2R 2LS

Tel: 020 7836 5454
Fax: 020 7836 1799
www.kcl.ac.uk

London Business School
Sussex Place
Regents Park
London NW1 4SA
Tel: 020 7262 5050
Fax: 020 7724 7875
www.london.edu

London School of Economics and Political Science
Houghton Street
London WC2A 2AE
Tel: 020 7405 7686
Fax: 020 7831 1684
www.lse.ac.uk

London School of Hygiene and Tropical Medicine
Keppel Street
London WC1E 7HT
Tel: 020 77636 8636
Fax: 020 7436 5389
www.lshtm.ac.uk

Queen Mary and Westfield College
Mile End Road
London E1 4NS
Tel: 020 7882 5555
Fax: 020 7882 5556
www.qmw.ac.uk

School of Oriental and African Studies
Thornhaugh Street
Russell Square
London WC1H OXG
Tel: 020 7637 2388
Fax: 020 7436 4211
www.soas.ac.uk

School of Pharmacy
29–39 Brunswick Square
London WC1N 1AX
Tel: 020 7753 5800
Fax: 020 7753 5829
www.ulsop.ac.uk

University College London
Gower Street
London WC1E 6BT
Tel: 020 7679 2000
Fax: 020 7679 3001
www.ucl.ac.uk

Colleges and institutes of higher education
Anglo European College of Higher Education
13–15 Parkwood Road
Boscombe
Bournemouth BH5 2DF
Tel: 01202 436 200
Fax: 01202 436 312
www.aecc.ac.uk

Bath College of Higher Education
Newton Park
Bath BA2 9BN
Tel: 01225 873 701
Fax: 01225 874 123
www.bathspa.ac.uk

Bedford College of Higher Education
Cauldwell Street
Bedford MK42 9AH
Tel: 01234 291 000
Fax: 01234 342 674
www.bedford.ac.uk

Bishop Grosseteste College
Lincoln LN1 3DY
Tel: 01522 527 347
Fax: 01522 530 243
www.bgc.ac.uk

Buckinghamshire College
Queen Alexandra Road
High Wycombe HP11 2JZ
Tel: 01494 522 141
Fax: 01494 524 392
www.bcuc.ac.uk

Canterbury Christchurch College
North Holmes Road
Canterbury CT1 1QU
Tel: 01227 767 700
Fax: 01227 470 442
www.canterbury.ac.uk

Central School of Speech and Drama
Embassy Theatre
Eton Avenue
London NW3 3HY
Tel: 0207 722 8183
Fax: 0207 722 4132
www.cssd.ac.uk

University College, Chester
Parkgate Road
Chester CH1 4BJ
Tel: 01244 375 444
Fax: 01244 373 379
www.chester.ac.uk

University College, Chichester
College Lane
Chichester PO21 1HR
Tel: 01243 816 000
Fax: 01243 816 080
www.ucc.ac.uk

Cumbria Institute of Arts
Brampton Road
Carlisle CA3 9AY
Tel: 01228 400 300
Fax: 01228 514 491
www.cumbria.ac.uk

Dartington College of Arts
Higher Close
Totnes TQ9 6EJ
Tel: 01803 862 224

Fax: 01803 861 666

www.dartington.ac.uk

Edge Hill College of Higher Education
St Helens Road
Ormskirk L39 4QP
Tel: 01695 575 171
Fax: 01695 579 997
www.edgehill.ac.uk

Edinburgh College of Art
Lauriston Place
Edinburgh EH3 9DF
Tel: 0131 221 6027
Fax: 0131 221 6028
www.eca.ac.uk

University College, Falmouth
Woodlane
Falmouth TR11 4RA
Tel: 01326 211 077
Fax: 01326 213 880
www.falmouth.ac.uk

Glasgow School of Art
167 Renfrew Street
Glasgow G3 6RQ
Tel: 0141 353 4500
Fax: 0141 353 4528
www.gsa.ac.uk

Harper Adams University College
Edgmond

Newport TF10 8NB
Shropshire
Tel: 01952 820 820
Fax: 01952 814 783
www.harper-adams.ac.uk

Newman College of Higher Education
Genners Lane
Bartlley Green
Birmingham B32 3NT
Tel: 0121 476 1181
Fax: 0121 476 1196
www.newman.ac.uk

University College, Northampton
Boughton Green Road
Northampton NN2 7AL
Tel: 01604 735 500
Fax: 01604 720 636
www.northampton.ac.uk

North Devon College
Old Sticklepath Hill
Barnstaple EX31 2BQ
Tel: 01271 45291
Fax: 01271 388121
www.ndevon.ac.uk

North East Wales Institute of Higher Education
Plas Coch
Mold Road
Wrexham LL112AW
Tel: 01978 290 666

Fax: 01978 290 008
www.newi.ac.uk

Norwich City College
Ipswich College
Norwich NR2 2LJ
Tel: 01603 660 011
Fax: 01603 760 326
www.ccn.ac.uk

Queen Margaret University College
Clerwood Terrace
Edinburgh EH12 8TS
Tel: 0131 317 3000
Fax: 0131 317 3256
www.qmuc.ac.uk

Further Reading

TRAVEL GUIDES
Great Britain, Lonely Planet Publications, London.
The Rough Guide to Britain, Rough Guide, London.
British Hotels, Inns and Other Places, Alastair Sawday, Alastair
   Sawday Publishing.
Good Pub Guide, Good Guides, London.
Bike Britain: Cycling from Land's End to John O'Groats, Paul
   Salter, Epic Guide.

TRAVEL WRITING
Notes from a Small Island, Bill Bryson, Swan Publishing, London.
*UK on a G-string: Adventures of the World's First and Worst Door-
   to-door Busker*, Justin Brown, Summersdale Publishers, London.

OTHER STUDENT GUIDES
*The 'Guardian' University Guide: What to Study, Where to Study and
   How to Make Sure You Get There*, Atlantic Books.
The Good University Guide, Sunday Times, London.
The Ultimate University Ranking Guide, Trotmans, London.
Cheeky Guide to Student Life, Cheeky Guides, Brighton.
Critical Thinking for Students, Roy van den Brink-Budgen, How To
   Books, Oxford.
Make Exams Easy, Mike Evans, How To Books, Oxford.
Writing an Assignment, Pauline Smith, How To Books, Oxford.
*The Essential Student Cookbook: 400 Budget Recipes to Leave Home
   with*, Cas Clarke, Headline Publishers, London.
The Student's Guide to Exam Success, Eileen Tracy, Open
   University Press,
Essential Study Skills: The Complete Guide to Success at University,
   Sandra Sinfield and Tom Burns, Sage Publications.

Students' Money Matters: The Indispensable Guide to Student Finance, Gwenda Thomas, Trotmans, London.

You might find it useful to have:

A general UK map.
A map of the UK with universities listed on it along with the nearest airports and ports.
A British Rail map.
A National Express map.

Index

accommodation, 167
accommodation agencies *see*
    letting agencies
AIDS, 124
airlines, 61, 62, 63, 64
airports, 61, 62, 63, 64
air travel, 61, 68
alcohol, 37
APEX, 66, 67
application, 5
    forms
        immigration, 84, 85
        universities, 7, 8
        visas, 78, 96
art galleries, 22
ATMs *see* cash machines

British
    customs and habits, 24
    people, 20
    slang, 26
bank accounts, 141
bank holidays, 59
bank notes, 29
banks, 141, 142, 146
bicycles, 71
book shops, 39
British Accreditation Council
    (BAC), 3
British Council, 6

budgeting, 148
building societies, 143
bureau de change, 29
BUSA, 164
buses, 64, 67

catering, 159
car
    buying, 69
    hiring, 70
    insuring, 35
cash machines, 31
CDs/DVDs, 40, 152
chemist *see* pharmacist
cheques, 143, 147
    clearing, 8
cinemas, 56
Citizens Advice Bureau, 133,
    134, 138, 157, 175, 176, 181,
    184
clearing (UCAS), 8
climate *see* weather
clothes, 37
clothing sizes, 38
colleges 97
    of further education (CFE),
    3
computers, 156
consulates 97
contraception, 121

contracts
  accommodation, 175
  work/employment, 134
council tax, 179
counselling, 123, 156
credit cards, 32
credit checks, 48
current account, 143, 147
customs, 24
customs allowance, 83
cycles/cycling, 71

debit cards, 32
dentists, 120
department stores, 37
dialling codes, 45
diesel, 152
directory enquiries, 46
discount cards, 41
doctor, 118
dress code, 55
driving
  laws/regulations, 68, 70
  learning, 69
  licence, 69
  test, 69
drugs, 59
dry cleaning, 40
DVDs, 40, 152

eating out, 54
electrical goods, 39
electricity, 36
embassies 97
emergency services, 49

employment, 128
employment agencies, 130
English language requirements,
  9
English language support, 157
entertainment, 55
EU students, 11
exams, 162
exchange rates, 30

fast food, 54
fees, 11
festivals, 56
flying to the UK, 61
flying within the UK, 65
food
  eating out, 54
  prices, 152
  shopping, 36
fully catered accommodation,
  168
funding *see* scholarships

galleries, 22
gas *see* utilities
gay and lesbian, 56, 164
geography, 21
graduation, 163

halls of residence, 167
harassment, 182
health, 116
health issues, 124
Highway Code, 68
holidays

entitlement, 134
public *see* bank holidays
host, 171
houses, 172
housing advice, 180

IELTS *see* English language
  requirements
internet, 49, 159
immigration *see also* visas
  advice, 91
  control, 81
  issues, 90
  offices, 81, 86, 87, 88, 89
  problems, 91
Immigration Advisory Service
  (IAS), 91
income tax, 133
insurance
  cars, 35
  health, 122
  house contents, 173
  travel, 35
internships, 129

jobs *see* employment

landlord, 176, 180, 181
laundry, 40
legal advice *see* Citizens Advice
  Bureau
lesbian *see* gay and lesbian
letting agencies, 172, 173
liquor *see* alcohol

magazines, 53

maps, 53
markets, 36
mobile phones, 47
money, 29
movies, 56
music festivals, 57
museums, 22

National Health Service
  (NHS), 117
national insurance, 131
newspapers, 52
NHS direct, 119
NHS 24, 119

opticians, 120
overdrafts, 148
overstaying, 90

pay phones/public phones, 45
petrol, 152
pharmacies, 37
police, 49
police registration, 83, 84, 154
postgraduate
  application, 8
  funding, 12, 13, 14
post office, 32
preparing to leave, 190, 191
prices, 152
prohibited goods, 83
public holidays (*see* bank
  holidays)
pubs, 55

racism, 21, 163

radio, 50
registration
   courses/university, 153, 154
   health, 154
   police, 154
religion, 58, 163
rent, 171
restaurants, 54

safety, 50
   tips, 72
savings account, 143, 147
Schengen, 93
scholarships, 12, 13, 14
sea travel, 65
self-catering accommodation,
   169
semester, 161
shipping, 190
shoe sizes, 43
shopping, 36
slang words, 26, 27, 28
speed limits, 68
sports, 164
storage, 189
Students' Union, 159
study methods, 161
supermarkets, 36

tax, 132, 133
tax forms, 135, 136
taxis, 72

telephone, 43
television, 51
television licence, 52
tickets, 73
time, 42
time differences, 43
TOFEL (*see* English language
   requirements)
trains, 64, 66
travel, 61, 65
travel agencies, 73
travellers' cheques, 141
tutors, 157

UCAS, 4, 7, 8
UKCOSA, 92
undergraduate courses, 7
university rankings, 5
utilities, 36

vaccinations, 123
VAT, 193
visas, 76, 77, 78
visa service, 95
visiting students, 10, 11
voluntary work, 164

weather, 58
weights and measures, 43
weapons, 60
work (*see* employment)